Chasing Your Destiny

"See Your God-Given Dream and Run After It"

Kara Mankey

Edited By
Monica Koldyke Miller

For my family,

Jimmy, I love how God made you with a sacrificial and servant's heart. You're a great man and I'm thankful I get to venture this journey of life with you!

Kenzie, the heart of Jesus shines through you. You're strong, steadfast, and compassionate.

Mason, your fun-loving personality is contagious. You find joy and blessings in the small things.

Maddy, you have a heart for worship and are a truth teller.

Acknowledgements

First I want to thank my Lord and Savior, Jesus Christ. Thank you for walking me through the mountaintops and valleys of life. You've changed my life and pulled me out of the pit because you love me. Thank you for showing me your Unfailing Love and giving me a story to share with the Nations. I was once in chains and you set me free. You overcame and claimed victory for me. Thank you for not giving up on me. Your love is sweeter than life and as long as I live, I'll glorify you. You are my hearts desire. This life is nothing without you. Thank you and I love you with all my heart.

Second, I want to thank my amazing husband, Jimmy. Thanks for your continued support and encouragement while walking the path of my destiny. There was sacrifice for our entire family, but you encouraged me to run after Jesus with all my heart. I'm truly grateful you believed in me and encouraged me to keep dreaming. Thank you for letting me use our family stories to fill the pages of this book. I'm blessed with the best family in the world!

Makenzie, Mason, and Maddy, run after the Lord with your whole being. Don't look to the left or to the right. Keep your eyes fixed on Jesus. He's your prize. Be confident with your identity in Him. He has great plans for you. Go after your destiny, and live your life with no regrets!

Love you to Heaven and back,

Mom

Contents

Introduction: Journey

Destiny and *Purpose*. How many times are these words used in our everyday conversations? What does it mean? Have you ever wondered what your specific *destiny, calling, or purpose* is on earth?

We can spend our entire lives searching for meaning and never find it. As humans, it's "normal" to seek our purpose in life. We want to know we are being helpful to others, performing our assignment, and contributing to society. This desire is instilled in us at birth. We want to find the place where we're investing into life, giving back, and helping make a difference.

Visualize a 1,000-piece puzzle. Each piece is different and yet necessary to see the completed picture. The same is true with mankind. God has a multi-billion-piece puzzle and each person represents a different part. To view the image in its entirety, it's crucial everyone finds where they fit.

First, we must realize we are unique; no other piece is exactly like us. Second, we were created to fit together with other pieces. Only when all the pieces are united as one, can we see the image God is creating. What a blessing, the Creator of the universe made each person with distinct characteristics and for a specific purpose.

So, how do we find where we fit, what our role is, and meaning in life?

For years, I had the misconception that my destiny was a single assignment. I wanted to figure out my purpose, do it, and then check my list as completed. I believed God would be pleased I'd discovered my destiny. I could then live the rest of my life for my own pleasure.

I'm going to be honest. I've had many misunderstandings about my life journey. The Lord has walked me through multiple mountaintops and valleys to reveal His truth to me.

Five years ago, I caught a glimpse of my destiny. I had a vision and saw the words, *Unfailing Love 1 John 4:19*. During the vision, the Lord spoke to me, telling me to go back to school. I needed to earn my Family Nurse Practitioner (FNP) degree because I would be opening a clinic. I instinctively knew this clinic would be a significant part of my destiny.

I interpreted this to mean I should open a clinic, immediately. I didn't realize there would be a long journey ahead of me. The logo and words I'd written down would represent my vision for years to come. I didn't know it'd include four-years of college, life lessons, and painful heart refinement.

I've since learned that destiny refers to a *process*, and when we choose to be led by the Holy Spirit, we are walking the *path of our destiny*. It's a long, winding, undulating road we get to walk everyday, with Jesus. Don't rush through and race for the destination. Instead, enjoy the voyage and daily treasures you find along the way.

This book is a reflection of my journey and the ups and downs I've encountered. I thought when I signed-up to follow Jesus, I'd coast on easy street. Life would always be glorious and on the mountaintop. That's a false reality. This book is a testimony of the struggles, challenges, and opposition I've faced as I ventured on my treasure hunt. It's the real-life, raw, and messy side of me. I never knew how flawed I was until I began walking my journey with Jesus.

Despite your circumstances, be encouraged and know God has a specific assignment for you. Things happen and we all have a past, but He still chose you from the beginning. He spoke words of purpose and destiny over you as He knit you in your mother's womb. Walking your destiny doesn't mean you're perfect or have it all together. It means you've received the mercy and grace of God and have surrendered to allow the power of the Holy Spirit to work through you. He created you to be a chosen people for Him and set apart for His eternal purposes.

Life is a journey waiting to be discovered. It's the most exhilarating ride you'll ever take. Come as you are, rest under the shadow of the Father's wings, and "Chase Your Destiny."

Blessings,

Kara

Treasure Hunt

In my early twenties, I traveled on my first overseas mission trip. I went with a team from our church to Costa Rica. I was excited and had multiple ideas of how to help these people. Globally, they were among the poorest of poor.

The local river had many different uses: drinking, bathing, washing clothes, and waste. They lived in houses the size of an average American bathroom, made of cardboard and pieces of wood. Two to nine people occupied each house, sleeping on dirt floors with blankets and a half-inch mattress.

The villages had open electrical wires running from shanty houses to a nearby power source. Wires hung four to six feet off the ground. I'm not tall, but I had to duck a few times while passing low electrical wires. As my head sunk between my shoulders, I prayed the open splices and sparks wouldn't catch my fly away hairs. It was hot and humid. Connection with a spark or electrical wire wouldn't have been a pretty sight.

My heart broke for these people. How could they live in houses with dirt floors? They bathed with the same water they drank from. How could they eat the same thing everyday and not have snacks? How did their children survive without the internet, television, and video games? Their clothes were old and worn. Most didn't have shoes. How did they survive without this stuff? I was a young American girl, ready to help. Maybe, I could donate shoes, clothes, candy, and toys. Would that help them?

For one week, I accompanied these precious people in their daily routines. I realized they were peaceful and happy despite their living conditions. They were happy because of the people in their lives. I mistakenly believed they were miserable because they didn't have material possessions. I realized I was full of lip service. Growing up, I'd been taught morals and manners. I knew politically correct answers. I'd voiced that God and family defined me, but those were empty words. My heart revealed its true colors. I now recognized the stronghold material possessions had on my life. I realized how selfish and inconsiderate I really was.

I was a spoiled American with everything at my fingertips. If I didn't feel like cooking, I'd go to my parents, grandparents, or pick up fast food. Anything I wanted, I could go and buy. If I didn't have money, I could use a credit card and pay later. I lived in a society that felt entitled to things and demanded instant gratification.

These people struggled to meet their daily needs. Physically they had nothing, but I saw them approach God with a heart of gratitude and thanksgiving. How could they express such joy in their poverty? I complained because I wanted, but didn't get, a bigger house, ATV's, another pair of shoes, or a Caribbean vacation. I needed to be thankful I had a house, a family that loved me, blankets and pillows on my bed, enough food, and clean clothes. I'd been blind to the treasures and blessings right in front of me.

A trip to Costa Rica exposed the grip material possessions held in my heart. I'd believed "things" made me happy and defined my identity. However, material possessions only provided temporary joy. They brought happiness in the moment and next week, but eventually, the pleasure faded. Then, it would be time to buy the next trending item. It was a vicious cycle that kept repeating itself. Over time, it left me broke and feeling empty. I wanted what they had. I was tired of giving lip service. I wanted a pure heart. How could I shift my heart from materialistic desires to appreciation for what I had?

In my quiet time, I reflected on this revelation. I could feel something in my heart awaken, in a place I'd never before encountered. I became overwhelmed with shame and guilt. I began to cry. I felt like someone had turned on a faucet and water streamed from my eyes. My lips were quivering and I couldn't speak. My heart was laid open before the Lord. My emotions made me want to run and hide. How could I come before the Lord all messy and broken? I had to clean up and gather my composure first. The perfectionist in me didn't allow me showing my faults. I feared being a failure.

In my weakness, tears, and runny nose, Jesus came and gently removed my shame, guilt, and self-condemnation. He came like a loving parent to wipe away tears from His child's face. I felt His peace embrace my heart. He reassured me I was okay. He wasn't mad at me. He wasn't judging me, but He wanted to remove these delusions of materialism and perfectionism, and plant truth in my heart. His truth was love, grace, mercy, joy, gentleness, restoration, and hope.

This was the beginning of me seeing the messy places in my heart. It was painful, but I've never encountered the gentleness of the Lord like I did that day. I always believed 'religion,' was simply a list of do's and don'ts. I had braced to suffer a penalty for my flawed thinking. But I felt no condemnation. He met me in my brokenness and began healing me from the inside out. God revealed my initial intention of helping these beautiful people had been selfish. My underlying motives were about me being a hero, doing great things they didn't need or even desire. These pure hearted people flipped my world upside down. I realized I needed them more than they needed me!

After my time in Costa Rica, my heart overflowed! I'd never experienced that before. I wanted to be in that space everyday. I developed the idea that overseas mission work would keep my heart filled. I came home prepared to be a missionary.

I told Jimmy, my husband, "Let's sell everything and move overseas to be missionaries."

He looked at me with a puzzled look, as if thinking, "Who is this lady in front of me and where did my wife go?"

He gently replied, "Well, you can go on all the mission trips you want, but someone needs to stay home with the kids. I can do that."

I felt at a loss. I had encountered the heart of the Lord. I was ready to dash off and tell the world about Jesus. I wanted to quit my nursing career and go into ministry. But my husband didn't agree. Over the weeks and months, I tried repeatedly to convince Jimmy to look into missionary work, but he wasn't interested. My heart burned for missions and I couldn't contain it. How could I dim a flame the Lord had ignited?

Financially, we weren't in a position to leave for the mission field. I had student and vehicle loans, and we were living paycheck to paycheck. I knew for the time being God wanted us to *stay*. I continued with my daily commitments of being a mother, wife, daughter, nurse, and friend. But my soul still longed for something more. I thought it was mission work, but maybe the Lord had something else in mind. I continued to spend time with Him, praying and reading scripture. I was seeking and waiting for an answer.

Within the next six months, I encountered a deeper understanding of Jesus's character and His love for me. I participated in a women's bible study at church. I'd always viewed God as a distant father, who made rules, and I had to follow them or I'd receive His judgment. Now I met wonderful women who gave me insight into their intimate relationship with Him. I heard the messy sides of their lives, but realized God was always there loving them in the midst of it.

Up to this point in my life, my Christian walk had been similar to a checklist. I made sure I had more checks on the good side than the bad. I never knew of the relational side of the Lord. It boggled my mind that He wanted to be in relationship with me. I didn't know how to walk in relationship with people, let alone the King of Kings. That notion felt intimidating, terrifying, yet a little exciting. I desired to know true intimacy and relationship with Jesus. I began studying the Bible, which opened my heart even more. I wanted the Holy Spirit to encounter me again and again.

A few weeks later, I recall standing beside our oldest daughter's crib. I stared at her. She looked delicate and precious. I felt a love cut deep to my core. No words could express it. I knew no matter what the future held, I'd always love her unconditionally. In the stillness of that moment, I felt a rush of peace over my mind and body. I felt as light as a feather, as if time had stopped.

I closed my eyes and I heard the Lord say, *I love you more than that.* I'd never heard the voice of the Lord before, but it came through my mind like a thought. I knew it wasn't my own. It was Jesus! The gentleness of the Holy Spirit embraced me. I knew it was real.

That encounter left me to hunger and thirst for more of Him. I wanted a deeper level of understanding. I slowly surrendered my life to the Lord, and finger-by-finger, He freed my grip on my own dreams. I released my desire of leaving for overseas missions. I surrendered to His will. This was difficult because I like being in control. When I have an idea or a burning desire, I want to run with it and make it happen.

I discovered the more I let go, the more peace and freedom I felt. I realized we aren't to dim the flame within us, but we're to let it burn, forging a deep well within our soul. I began to learn the meaning of patience.

We weren't going overseas to be missionaries. I knew Jesus had a purpose for us here. I told the Lord, "I'll stay and wait. I'll let the flame burn within my soul for the process of refining. But please, put the brakes on in my mind, to allow me to focus on my current commitments. Help me be happy and joyful where I am." No matter how painful it was to stay, I decided to enjoy moments in life, like watching my children sleep.

Our *destiny, calling, and purpose* is something that's cultivated in us as we slow down, walk our journey with Jesus, and allow Him to transform our character on a daily basis. It doesn't happen in one moment, but in many moments that build on each other as we encounter the heart of the Lord.

In Costa Rica, I caught a glimpse of my destiny. I started the treasure hunt God designed and I'd received my first clue. I learned I had a heart for "***Serving and Loving Others***." It's an amazing discovery, because prior to this trip, I was selfish. Afterward, Jesus pulled out of me the treasure of service, which is the exact opposite.

I've heard the enemy call me spoiled, inadequate, rebellious, greedy, inpatient, and hateful. But the Lord said, *I call you blessed, worthy, more than enough, pure, steadfast, giving, thankful, gentle, patient, and loving.* Walking our destiny is a process of Him exchanging our ashes for beauty.

A few years ago, a dear friend had given me a prophetic word. "Treasure hunts and bounty abound for you."

That sounded amazing! I'm always up for an adventure. But I was more excited about the "bounty." At that time, I'd returned to college to obtain my FNP degree. I'd been working minimal hours, was married, and Jimmy and I had three little mouths to feed. Money was tight. I was ready for a bounty and I assumed it would be a financial blessing. I decided that's what we needed and wanted, so it had to be. As you read this book, you'll see I liked to make assumptions of what God wanted.

Well, that wasn't the case. The next couple of years passed and I still didn't see the "bounty" portion of it. As I'm typing, I received revelation about that word. *Know our bounty or pot of gold is the day we're no longer on this earth, but standing face to face with Jesus. He's our prize.*

No amount of money can buy that precious gift. The treasure hunt is about the journey, the relationships, finding the clues, and the adventure. Then, we'll piece all the clues together hearing Jesus say, *Well done, good and faithful servant.*

There are many stops along the way, but each one is necessary. In hindsight, we'll see His beautiful handiwork and how He's transformed our hearts and character. Count each step as a blessing. Enjoy the adventure. And then, take time to connect and invest with the people who are stationed along the voyage with you.

Seven years ago, staying home and not leaving for the mission field was my hidden blessing. I saw meaningful things that were nothing material, but the people the Lord placed in my life. I have a husband who adores me. I'm blessed with three beautiful children who love me and make me smile. They bring

19

out the best in me, especially when I start boiling inside and cannot contain it anymore. Soon, I'm yelling at the top of my lungs to quit nit picking at each other. In our house, we definitely have our moments, and that's okay. We're a family who loves, gives grace, laughs and cries together, forgives and forgets, and picks on each other. We have our ups and downs. Yet, those are the joys and treasured memories no one can take from us.

I remember the joy of listening to the patter of our kids' feet coming down the hallway, knowing they were going to squeeze their little behinds into our queen size bed. It was a tight fit, but joyful. We'd roll around, tickle each other, and hope no one fell off. I can think back to when my son would convince my husband to hold me down so he could tickle me. I would get so frustrated. I'd be yelling and laughing, while trying to break free from my husband's grip. Recalling the sound of my son's little chuckle still warms my heart.

Those are life's blessings and treasures that money can't buy. Slow down and realize there's a long journey ahead. Don't race for the pot of gold, but enjoy every step and uncover your destiny!

Lord, I pray for grace and patience to know there is a long journey ahead of us. Help us to appreciate our blessings on a day-to-day basis. Give us a Kingdom perspective and appreciation for the true treasures and joys in life, not material possessions. Thank you for turning our ashes into something beautiful. We rejoice because you call us worthy and have a calling and purpose over all of our lives. I pray for a fire within our souls to pursue you and your heart and enjoy this crazy adventure you have destined for us!

Blessings,

Kara☺

Surrender

The summer between my seventh and eighth grade year, I enrolled in summer church camp. I made new friends, went swimming, had good food, and sat around a campfire; but most importantly, I met Jesus. During worship and late night conversations with campers and counselors, I felt valued and loved. I learned about the love of Christ, and during an open invitation, I accepted Him as my Lord and Savior.

I continued through my eighth grade year encountering the heart of Jesus. I attended public school. During class we often had journaling assignments. As I re-read those journal entries, I found I'd answer the leading question, but somehow my answer would shift to an eternal perspective. Almost every page became filled with Jesus or Heaven. My mind had been consumed with God.

That was the first time I'd surrendered my heart to the Lord. It became a pivotal moment and the beginning of learning to be led by the Holy Spirit. Yet, I was far from perfect, and naive of the temptations that would later cross my path.

In my teenage years, especially during college, I began to withdraw from church and spending time in prayer. My prayers shifted from being heartfelt and meaningful, to throwing petitions heavenward because I needed help. "I don't want to study, but I want a good grade on my test."

Trust me, these kinds of prayers don't work. It was selfish and all about me. I didn't want to put forth the effort, but I wanted to reap a bountiful harvest.

The Kingdom isn't designed to work that way. God doesn't teach us enabling or entitlement. He walks us through life, developing a desire within us to go after the things of His heart. He wants us to choose Jesus and love Him more than His blessings. God tests our motives. We have to put some skin into the game, move our feet, and run wholeheartedly after Him. Are we willing to give up things of this life to know the deep parts of the Father?

My children are in gymnastics. It's a great sport physically, emotionally, and mentally. If they want to learn a skill, they must put in the work to achieve their goal. The same is true with the Kingdom. God births our desires and dreams, but we have to labor to reach it. The Holy Spirit guides us, but we must do our part. When we desire the heart of Jesus, He blesses everything we do. Maybe not the way we envisioned, but in a way that's most beneficial.

I truly believe the saying, "we reap what we sow." I'm good at math. It comes natural for me. In 2003, I worked to obtain my Associate in Nursing, to be a Registered Nurse (RN). I'd also taken classes for my Bachelor's degree, having tested out of some basic classes. I included statistics, thinking it'd be a breeze. Well, I put forth little effort and consequently, received my first D. I was mostly an A student, so I felt blindsided. I tried talking my teacher into figuring a way to earn a C, but she told me there was nothing she could do. I'd have to retake the class.

By receiving this grade, I'd been put on academic probation with the nursing department. I couldn't take any nursing classes the next semester. Graduation was now delayed another semester. I was furious! I felt like an idiot and a failure. Mostly, I was ashamed. I threw a couple prayers to heaven asking to graduate on time, but there was no divine intervention. The Lord didn't answer my prayers.

In hindsight, it was a blessing and exactly what I needed to refine my character to who God created me to be. I had drifted from that sacred place in eighth grade. I'd become more focused on partying, my boyfriend, and popularity status than my savior, redeemer, and lover of my heart.

One night, I was at Jimmy's house. He and a friend were watching a movie I didn't want to see. I went to the other room and began flipping through television channels. As I sat by myself, I felt a stillness come over me. I became oblivious to the television, and the noise faded. Without prompting, my current lifestyle streamed like a movie in my mind. I became painfully aware of my shameful ways. This wasn't the life I envisioned for myself. I felt humiliated and angry.

How could I let myself stray from that eighth grade encounter with Jesus? I had achieved some of the things I'd desired: the job, social status, and guy. But it left me feeling lonely, empty, greedy, entitled, selfish, and hateful. I hated myself. I hated who I had become. Deep within my heart, I no longer wanted to be that person. I felt in chains, with no way of breaking free. They were too heavy to lift. I felt exhausted living by the world's standards.

Feeling broken, my eyes welled up. I lay on my back and cried, "Lord, I can't live like this anymore! I've become someone I despise and I need you. I want to be the person you created me to be. I don't know how to get out of this mess. I feel stuck!"

The Lord impressed my heart, saying, *Kara, I'm with you and I love you. I'll give you a way out, but you need to stop drinking.*

In that moment, my heart again surrendered to Jesus. "Okay. I'm in, I'm all yours. Have your way with me."

This was a second chance for a new beginning. I surrendered to the Lord with a heart of repentance. Over the next year, the Lord drew me away from the crowds I hung out with, and Jimmy and I broke up. I started attending church. It was different from the church I grew up in and it was refreshing.

I now realized what I wanted. I wanted a family that loved deeply, enjoyed togetherness, went to church, and didn't live a party-centered life. Those were my new standards. But it wasn't achieved instantly. I still had a long journey ahead, a process of making choices that reflected the Kingdom. I stepped onto the path of my destiny, but deep inside my soul, I still missed and longed for one thing: Jimmy.

Jimmy and I had experienced more downs than ups our first two years of dating. Despite his tough-guy demeanor, I'd become acquainted to the gentle spirit and selfless side of his heart. I knew him to be a man of service and sacrifice, and I still longed for him. After a few months, we ran into each other and decided to give it another try.

This was the beginning of a new adventure and God blessed me. He'd given me one of the desires of my heart. Now, fourteen years later, we're becoming the family I always desired. It hasn't been an easy journey, but I'm grateful to have Jimmy by my side. Even when I pushed my desire for missions, he stood by me and loved me through it.

After my first trip to Costa Rica, I continued spending time with Jesus, family, and work; but my heart still longed for the mission field. Seven months later, Jimmy and I were given a mission opportunity. The earthquake in Haiti had just occurred. Our church planned to send teams for construction and medicine. I felt ecstatic because I had another opportunity to serve. Additionally, it would include the two professions Jimmy and I are experienced in. This possibility fueled a fire within my soul. This was my opportunity to convince Jimmy to come, and maybe he'd develop a love for mission work, too.

At the time, I'd been an RN for four years. I had experience working in large hospital intensive care units and in an oral surgeon's office. I enjoyed caring for people. My love for medicine had birthed true compassion. Whether dying with dignity or helping patients take steps with hope they'd walk again, I knew I could be of service.

Jimmy had worked construction for the past six years. He's a jack-of-all-trades and can build just about anything. I knew he had to come with me. We'd be in the presence of the Lord, away from the pressures of life, and serving in occupations we loved. I also had a hidden motive he'd change his mind and want to be an overseas missionary, once he experienced it himself.

We initially heard of the trip in February. I had eight months to convince Jimmy to come with me. I tried and tried, begged and begged, but his answer was still "no." After two months of trying, I stopped.

I prayed, "Lord, I'm going on this trip, I give Jimmy to you. If you want him to go, then you'll have to move his heart. I'm done trying to persuade him." I released Jimmy to the Lord. I was frustrated and exhausted. I continually prayed for grace and patience, giving God space to encounter Jimmy. I had to be okay whether he went or not. It was God's choice, not mine.

The begging and nagging stopped, but a few comments still slipped out. It was very hard for me to keep silent. Two months later at our group Bible study, we were discussing vacations; how they're necessary for marital time, but how it's hard to leave our kids.

All of a sudden, Jimmy said, "Yea, in a few months Kara and I are going to Haiti, and it'll be hard to leave our kids, but we know we're supposed to go."

I froze, my heart skipped a few beats. Had I heard him right? Could I hit rewind and play that again? I contemplated slapping my face to make sure I wasn't dreaming. I turned and looked at Jimmy. He looked into my eyes, smiled, and then gave me a simple nod.

Neither of us spoke while others continued the conversation, but I felt overwhelmed with joy and confidence in the power of the Holy Spirit. When Jesus wants something done, He's the one who moves people's hearts, not me!

We're both in. We're going to Haiti! We began writing support letters to family and friends and we received all our funding. Six weeks before we were scheduled to leave, I took a pregnancy test. It revealed two red lines. We were having our third child. We wanted another child, but planned to wait until after we returned from Haiti. Medically, it was recommended we take antimalarial and typhoid pills. These medications aren't safe during pregnancy. I wanted them out of my system before trying to become pregnant. Well, God had different plans. He was about to develop my faith muscles and strengthen my heart of surrender.

I questioned if I was supposed to go on this trip. Jimmy and I agreed not to tell anyone I was pregnant, until we knew if I'd be going. I couldn't handle everyone's concerns and opinions. I didn't want to back out because of fear, which is something I've always struggled with. I wanted a clear answer from the Lord.

I called my obstetrician and asked if there were alternatives to taking the medications. And, he replied, "No, it would be safest for the baby, if you didn't go." Although, he gave me honest medical advice, it didn't sit well with my spirit.

Jimmy and I prayed, and I pursued God deeply for an answer. During one of my devotions, I came across **Mark 16:15-20**. Jesus was getting ready to ascend to Heaven, and told his disciples, "You will pick up snakes and drink deadly poison and it will not harm you." This resonated within my spirit. When scripture comes alive and speaks to you, you feel it within your soul. Something moved in me, and "my knower" just knew I'd received my answer.

I immediately called Jimmy and told him and he replied, "Alright, we're going. If the Lord says you'll be okay, then you'll be okay."

We were both going to Haiti. Ten weeks pregnant and no preventative medications, let's do it! To Jimmy it was black and white, but I still had fears and doubts.

Over the next month, I had to ground myself in prayer and resolve that, 'Yes, I'm going, and no, I'm not taking preventative medicine.'

As we told family and friends, the same concerns arose, and I heard over and over, "You're not still going to Haiti, are you?"

My convictions were grounded and settled. Jimmy and I responded with confidence, "Yes!" We then shared our confirmation story.

Surrender. I've learned surrender isn't a one-time decision or a few significant moments. It's a daily choice. No matter where I am on my path, every morning I have to choose to wake up, abandon my own plans and agenda, and say, "Good morning Lord. Here I am. My life and heart are yours today." I must lay my flesh at the foot of the cross, and daily surrender to what He has for me every moment of every day. I have to choose the Kingdom, not the ways of the world.

As Jimmy and I traveled to Haiti, we surrendered our unborn child to God. I knew Jesus said, "Go," but I had to choose to surrender my fears, insecurities, and medical knowledge before Him. In this situation, medicine said *No*, but Jesus said *Yes*!

Our week in Haiti was amazing. And, our precious daughter was born healthy and perfect, six and a half months later. Today she's an active, healthy five year old, with much sass and life.

Haiti was a significant time in our lives. It was another pivotal moment. During our trip, Jimmy and I served on our specialty teams, but we also had time to serve alongside each other. There's nothing more precious than serving and loving others alongside your spouse. During our times apart, I worked in the medical clinic. The Holy Spirit kept nudging me out of my comfort zone. I began to ask people if I could pray for them. There was a language barrier. Interpreters weren't always available, and I didn't speak Creole. I used hand motions to ask patients if I could pray for them. I then spoke my prayers in English. We didn't understand each other, but I could feel the connection of our hearts. Afterward, these precious people would hug me or tightly squeeze my hand as a means of appreciation.

By the power of the Holy Spirit, I served and loved them as Jesus demonstrated to his disciples. He reached out for the broken hearted. Not necessarily just the poor or in a particular location, but those whose hearts longed for connection, love, and something genuine.

This was the first time I'd integrated medicine and ministry. It was foreign to me, but it felt right! This new concept replaced my belief I had to be on a mission trip to encounter Jesus in my work. Being a missionary still burned within me, but my perspective changed. I again surrendered my plans for overseas mission work. I let God give me a new understanding for the term 'missionary.' I realized my job as a nurse would be my platform for ministry. I'm so thankful I surrendered my unborn child, fears, insecurities, doubts, and agenda because on this trip I received the next piece of my treasure hunt, "*Medicine was my Ministry*!"

I was clueless to what this meant, or where my next step would be, but I found it fulfilling. I continued to keep my eyes fixed on Jesus and walked the path of my destiny. I encountered the Lord moving in my life and my soul hungered for more!

Lord, I pray no matter where we are in life, we fall face down before the foot of the cross and surrender our fears and the desires of our flesh to receive the blessings of freedom, love, grace, mercy, joy, and peace. Lord open the eyes of our hearts to receive the assignment and the courage, desire, strength, and discernment to walk in it! Stir within us a hunger to run after your heart with our entire being! Thank you for giving us grace as we learn to surrender to you and

your ways!

Blessings,

Kara☺

Glimpse

After our trip to Haiti, I started working at the hospital in our small hometown community. I enjoyed serving people I knew, and those I could make a familial connection with. Working at the hospital, the Lord started to teach me how to integrate medicine and ministry.

The Spirit of the Lord began to nudge my heart to ask patients if I could pray for them. I didn't pray with every patient, just those Jesus laid on my heart. This wasn't standard practice at our hospital, and they didn't teach this in nursing school. It felt really awkward. The first time I felt the Holy Spirit's nudge was with an older Amish gentleman.

The doctor came in to discuss a treatment, and I could tell by my patient's expression, he didn't comprehend the plan. The doctor's terminology was difficult to understand and the plan was complicated.

After the doctor left, I asked, " Do you have any questions?"

He gave me a blank stare.

In terms I believed he'd understand, I summarized the treatment, assuring him we'd take care of him. I could tell he found comfort in my words. As I looked at the Amish gentleman, he gave me the sweetest smile. But my spirit felt uneasy, for I recognized his emotion. It was fear. My heart broke for him.

I began a conversation with him about his profession, family, and hobbies. In the middle of the discussion a thought came that said, "Pray for him."

I acted like I didn't hear it and I continued to give my patient my undivided attention. The thought came again, only a little louder, and repeated the same thing. Inwardly, I looked to the Lord and said, "You have to be kidding me."

The patient was sitting on the side of the hospital bed, his feet dangled, and I stood next to him appearing to be engaged in conversation. I made good eye contact and muttered an occasional "Yea, uh-uh, oh," to assure him I was listening. All the while, I was wrestling with God.

I came up with every excuse why I shouldn't pray with this patient. "Many Amish practice Christianity, but not all of them. His daughter's in the room, I don't want an audience. I feel stupid, what do I say? I'm a nurse, not a pastor." In an instant, the Lord spoke five words that shook me to my core.

Are you ashamed of me?

My heart sank. As my stomach knotted, I took a deep sighing breath and replied, "No, I'll do it."

I struggled to ask if I could I pray for him.

I loved Jesus. Why was it so difficult to step out and ask this patient if I could release the heart of Jesus over him? What was I afraid of?

I had to pump myself up, telling myself, "Do it. Step into your fear and ask him. What's the worst he could say, No?" My heart was racing, palms sweating, and my entire body shook.

Finally, words slowly rolled off my tongue. "S-S-S-Sir, I'm not sure if you practice Christianity, but I can sense you're concerned about your treatment plan. Would you be willing to let me pray for you?"

He looked at me, gave me a huge smile, and said, "I'd love that."

The Lord showed up. After all my wrestling and wanting to run the other way, He showed up and encountered the heart of this gentleman. It was a precious moment and a foundational rock for me to stand on. This was the start of me stepping out and praying with patients. It was a blessing and I began to feel valued.

I'd grown up hearing God had a plan for me. But I carried doubt and unbelief He'd use a sinner like me. I was far from being the "picture-perfect Christian." I'd partied in college, lived with my boyfriend, and had two kids before getting married. I didn't feel worthy to have a calling on my life besides being a mother, wife, and nurse. My goal was to teach my children to live life in the right order; date, get married, then have children.

Praying inconspicuously over patients during my shifts built up my confidence. I could see God moving. No patient ever said 'no.' As I witnessed the Holy Spirit encounter him or her, I saw genuine smiles after every prayer. Sometimes their eyes welled with tears, and they'd hug me, or squeeze my hands, saying, "Thank you!"

The Lord restored their hope. People were grateful for my bold and courageous offers of prayer. I started to see purpose for my life. He did have a plan after all.

I'm not proud of my past poor choices, but it's my testimony of God's grace. It's a Cinderella story of a broken, overlooked, and lost girl whom God restored. He took me from poverty to royalty. I pursued Him on a daily basis by prayer, worship, and reading scripture.

I started to journal and practiced hearing God's voice. I've only heard the Lord's voice audibly a couple times, which occurred in dreams. His voice usually comes to me as a thought. I started by asking Jesus "yes" and "no" questions. Eventually, I learned how to distinguish between His words, my own thoughts, and the lies from enemy. I discovered when the enemy spoke, he made me feel fear, doubt, unbelief, anger, or jealousy.

Hearing God's voice was a "spiritual muscle" the Holy Spirit taught me to use. This ability was still in its infant stages, but it formed the basis for me to start on.

I also began learning about the heart of Jesus for me and other people. Everything centers around love. Love Jesus and love the people around you. The more I pursued the Lord, the more I felt a new desire rise up within my heart. I didn't know what it was, but I knew He had something more for me. This feeling continued for a few months. I kept asking God, "What are you birthing within me?" I received no reply, but I kept seeking and asking for months.

There came a day I couldn't take it anymore. I felt desperate and needed an answer. I lay face down on my living room floor with my arms out to my side. Worship music played softly in the background. My Bible lay open in front of me and I rested my forehead on it. Initially, I felt angry and frustrated because the Lord hadn't answered me. With irritation in my voice I said, "Lord, what do you want with me? I've been asking and seeking, but you haven't answered me. I need to know because this burning desire within me won't go away. You need to answer me or take the desire away!" He didn't say a word. I lay there, listened to the music, and I felt my mind begin to still. My anger and irritation ebbed and I began to weep. Tears soaked the pages of my Bible, and I surrendered my heart. "Lord, here I am. Whatever you want, I'll do it."

In that moment, I felt his presence come over me. My body felt weightless as if I could float. For the first time in months, my mind became clear and unburdened. There was nothing on my mind. I listened to the music and felt overwhelming peace. I heard the Lord say, *You're going to start a clinic.*

I could feel my mind shifting. I saw myself in a desert with a few trees off in the distance. I stood in the door of a building. The building was made of tree trunks, and I instinctively knew I wasn't in the United States. People were lined up outside the clinic waiting to be seen for medical concerns. In the vision, I looked happy and I could physically feel my joy and peace.

I said, "Lord, what kind of clinic?" He showed me a logo that read *Unfailing Love 1 John 4:19.*

I opened my eyes and realized I was in my living room. I jumped up off the floor and without hesitation ran to grab a paper and pencil. I sketched the logo to the best of my ability on a post-it note and stuck it on the side of my refrigerator. I went back to my Bible and looked up **1 John 4:19** and it read, **"We love because He first loved us."**

I sat on my living room floor wondering, "Did this really happen or did my mind just make it up?" Out loud, I said, "Lord, how am I going to do this?"

He said, *Go back to school.*

I responded with frustration. "Didn't we try this already? It didn't really work out."

Three years before, I'd enrolled in a FNP program. I had been registered in a summer Pathophysiology class, and I was trying to figure out how the fall semester would work with my schedule. I'd recently started a new job at an oral surgeon's office while pregnant with our second child. Financially, I needed to work full-time, which meant I worked four and a half days per week. My work days and hours weren't flexible enough for a college schedule. I'd wanted to be a nurse practitioner, but after finishing the summer course, I realized the timing wasn't right.

I explained this to the nursing department and they accepted my resignation. Later that week after declining the FNP program, I was in the shower having a conversation with the Lord. I received a message so profound, which resonates even today. "How do I know when the timing is right to return to school?" I asked.

Jesus had replied, *When you do it for the right reasons.*

At the time, that reply made me angry. "What do you mean?" I said. "I want to help people." The Lord didn't say a word. He let me sit with my anger. Over the next three years, the Holy Spirit took me on a journey and began the work of refining my heart. He did it by leading me to places that broke the heart of God, the mission field. Those experiences caused my desires to align with His; for the *right* reasons.

Initially, I wanted to be a nurse practitioner because they made good money, had good hours and benefits, and our family would be financially set. There's nothing wrong with wanting to be financially secure, but my focus had been about me, not the heart of the Father. I was too busy looking at the material possessions I could have with an increased salary. I didn't possess the motives to help and invest in people's lives. I was more concerned with my monetary status and the vacations we could take. I'd been blind to the poverty and brokenness in our world.

My travels to Costa Rica and Haiti were life-altering trips. My heart shifted into alignment with God's. In my initial steps on my treasure hunt with the Lord, I'd gathered my first clues. I could see my calling. I became willing to give up everything to have more of Him. Material possessions weren't important anymore. I desired to have a pure heart and to know the depths of the Father's heart.

As I died to the desires of my flesh, God released me to be a nurse practitioner. On that day, as I lay face down on my living room floor, the doorway to my heart's desire was finally opened. I now had the opportunity to walk through it. Jesus again repeated, *Go back to school.*

I said, "Okay Lord, I'll start the process."

My husband came home from work a few hours later and I told him about my encounter with Jesus. Jimmy smiled when I showed him the post-it note. "That's great. Do it. Go back to school. I'll help keep things in order around the house."

My husband is amazing because he's never experienced the Lord in visions, but he always believed mine. I've told Jimmy I appreciated him not putting me down or telling me I'm crazy. He explained it like this: "Kara, you've never been a good storyteller so I know it has to be real. The detail you explain, you can't make up something like that. Maybe I could, but you can't."

The next week, I applied online to the University of Saint Francis for their RN-MSN (Registered Nurse to Master of Science in Nursing) program. Part-time, the program would take me four years to complete. Graduation seemed out of reach, but I knew if I never started, I wouldn't finish. I had to move my feet and be ready to labor. My heart was set on the Father and His promise of the logo on the post-it note. I had to plant my feet at the starting line and get ready to "*Run my Race*."

Father, thank you for having a race for each of us to run. We each have our own lane with a prize at the end. I pray for dreams and visions over your children. Rise up desires within us to sit and dream with you. Thank you for being faithful and bringing our God-given dreams to fruition. You are the God who calls things that are not as though they are (Romans 4:17). You are a good Father who showers

blessings and favor upon us. I pray for endurance,
motivation, and perseverance as we run our race and chase
our destiny.
Blessings,
Kara ☺

Seasons

On this beautiful planet called earth, we have four distinct seasons. Winter, spring, summer, and fall. I love the change of seasons, and living in Indiana, I get to experience every one of them. Have you ever thought about what occurs in each season and how it's necessary for the process of life to occur? Preparing the soil, planting of seeds, growing, maturing, refining, and even death.

We savor weather associated with each season. We look out the window and see rain, sun, fog, or snow. We step outside and take a deep breath of the cool, dewy autumn morning or smell the freshness of budding flowers in the spring. We see our breath as we exhale in chilly winter air, and in summer, we feel the sun's warmth on our skin. Every season is different with its own conditions and its own beauty.

In winter, the ground is bare, frozen, and being renewed to prepare soil to birth new sprouts. This reminds me of my heart being exposed before the Lord. He reveals things inside

45

me that aren't aligned with Him. My heart feels open, vulnerable, and messy like sloshy, melting snow on the road. He's preparing the soil of my heart to nourish the seed He's going to plant within me. He wants it to take root and bloom into something beautiful. But the ground has to be ready and enriched. Although the road may appear messy, He's begun the cleansing process, so my heart has rich soil to care for the seed.

Spring is beautiful because everything starts out fresh and unspoiled. Plants and flowers begin sprouting from seeds that aren't visible. This reminds me that each of us has a chance for a new beginning. There's something working inside us we can't see. The Lord sows seeds within our hearts. He's waiting for us to yield to His water and sunshine, which allow the shoots to bloom. Eventually, we'll see the first fruits of His plantings.

Once summer arrives and the seedlings grow, it's time to reshape them. Water and sunshine are essential, but it's also a season for pruning. Pruning cuts off any branches that aren't blooming. This reminds of me of the Lord renewing my mind and heart. He shows me the parts of my life that aren't bearing fruit. Pruning is painful. That pain causes me to relinquish desires of my flesh. Summer is a season of learning to loosen my grip of control, allowing Jesus to mold me into a new creation.

In the fall, flowers wilt and leaves change color before falling to the ground. This reminds me of the continuing process of maturing. As you spiritually ripen, you'll become your own unique creation. You'll see who you are in Christ when your true colors emerge. Once you learn your identity, former ways of thinking and acting die and fall away. Though never perfect, Jesus continually transforms us. As soon as one round of 'heart work' is over, He begins another.

Walking in and out of spiritual seasons is a beautiful and necessary process to discover your true identity. Some seasons last days, weeks, months, or even years. Each one is essential to cultivating our character and walking in the fullness of who God created us to be. Along this walk, the Lord teaches lessons, strengthens our spiritual muscles, and refines us. As we recognize our uniqueness in Christ, we'll uncover our purpose and destiny. Entering into relationship with Jesus requires surrender, obedience, and a willingness to walk with Him wherever He leads. Relationship with Jesus is saying, "Lord, I love you and trust you with my life."

When starting Unfailing Love Clinic, I learned to clearly hear the voice of the Lord. I practiced for four years and became confident and grounded on His promises for my life and the clinic. My ego was getting pretty big. But, I didn't realize it until the Holy Spirit took me into a season of clothing myself in humility.

I was in my last semester of the FNP program. Our board had been planning how to launch the clinic and obtain the initial funding and resources. We still had no idea where the clinic would be located. In January, Jesus kept laying a building on my heart. He confirmed this with Bible verses and through a book I'd been reading. I told our board, and they said, "Okay, let's go for it."

We found a building, but it wasn't for sale. At this time, we'd just started our 501c3 (non-profit status) and didn't have funds. I experienced many negative emotions. I was an introvert and a people pleaser; I didn't like being in the forefront. I felt nauseated at the thought of making an offer.

Jesus reminded me of Joshua leading the Israelites through the Jordan River to enter the Promised Land **(Joshua 3:1-17)**. The river was high and the Israelites couldn't cross. God told Joshua to have the priests put their feet in the water. They obediently did so, and the river parted. The Israelites crossed the Jordan on dry ground and entered the Promised Land.

What if the priests hadn't been obedient and never put their feet in the water? They would've waited a long time or performed unnecessary labor to cross before entering the Promised Land. Yet, the priests stepped out in faith and a miracle happened. We'll never see the supernatural if we're not willing to move our feet and walk in faith.

My step-dad is a realtor and he knew those who owned the building. With his help, our team went and looked at the building. We agreed it was perfect. There was enough space for a team to practice medicine and ministry.

The property included a full-sized, unfinished basement. As I walked into the basement, the Lord whispered to me, *You'll give from your storehouse.* I felt confused, and said, "That's great. I receive that, but we don't have anything except prayer to give right now." I never heard Jesus reply, but I felt at peace and confident there was more to come.

Once we finished our inspection, our team joined hands. We stood in a circle and prayed over the building. Everyone agreed to make an offer. That's how the Kingdom works. When the Holy Spirit is leading a team to move, He confirms it with scripture and everyone is in agreement.

Everything except funding was now in alignment. We had no money in our bank account. I said, "Okay, let's step into the Jordan and watch the miraculous happen." We made an offer on the building mid February. In May, we would need to make a $5,000 deposit and by mid July, we had to have the full amount.

Over the course of those five months, I was a hot mess. I kept asking the Lord what was next, and how we would get funding. He'd said "no" to my inquiries on fundraising, "no" to grants, and now He wasn't giving further direction. The clinic received donations from friends and family, which helped obtain our initial funding.

Our deadline in May was closing in. We had half of our deposit. In prayer, I pleaded, "Lord, don't give us the deposit unless you're going to give us the full amount for the building." Two days before our deadline, we received donations to cover our deposit. I emailed our board and they all replied, "Put down the deposit."

I felt excited, yet nervous. I held onto God's seeming answer to my plea, "Don't give us the deposit if you're not going to give us the building." I didn't want to look like an idiot.

Once the deposit was made, we had six weeks to raise the balance of $145,000. Two weeks before our July deadline, we had a board meeting and we weren't anywhere close to our goal. Our team decided to wait it out.

Those were the longest two weeks of my life. I was scared and angry. I said, "Lord, why would you have us step out and make me feel uncomfortable? You know I don't like to be out in front, let alone be made a fool of. You have to show up! We've done everything you've asked. Where are you? What are we supposed to do?" I received no answer and no direction. I said, "Lord, I need a word. I need to know where to plant my feet."

A few nights later I went to a local church service. At the end of the service, the pastor had a prophetic word for two people. I instinctively knew one of the messages would be for me. I was in a crisis and had been pleading for an answer. I sat in the pew waiting for the pastor to describe whom he wanted to encourage. I was nervous, but ready to march up front to receive prayer. The pastor finished talking and there were two people who went up front, a man and myself.

The pastor prayed first for the man and he kept talking and talking. As I waited, I became overwhelmed with emotion. Fears of failure and rejection made me anxious to hear from the Lord. Finally, it was my turn.

The pastor placed his hand on my shoulder and prayed. He said, "Jesus says, you're in the hallway of life. It's a place of transition. There are no windows or light and it's dark. Things seem very scary and uncertain. Know it's not the final destination. It may be longer than what you thought, but stay with me. Keep your heart clean. The hallway is going to give you substance to build your testimony. Keep holding my hand because we're about to take a turn. Furniture, light, and blessings await. Be comfy and happy in this place. I'm going to position you to minister to more people. I'm building your platform to share your testimony; you'll have words of life to release to people. I will bring the people."

Suddenly, my knees felt weak. I began to cry. My chest heaved and my lips trembled. I felt helpless, but I knew I was safe in the Lord's presence. Being in the hallway is painful. It's dark, scary, and there are many unknowns. I couldn't see the door, let alone my next step.

One time, we'd taken our kids to Science Central (a center with hundreds of hands-on exhibits) where there was a house with tunnels built inside. This particular activity taught kids to use their sense of touch. You had to keep moving through the house and tunnels in total darkness. There was only one way you could go and you needed to feel your way through. My kids were little and wanted me to go with them. I tried getting out of it, but they insisted. Once we entered the darkness, I became fearful. I tried remaining calm, knowing I had to be brave for my children.

That lasted about sixty seconds, and then I cheated. I grabbed my cell phone and turned on the flashlight. Once the light came on, my panic disappeared. It didn't light the entire path or further ahead, but the next turn or ladder to climb. I could see what came next. Being in darkness and not seeing the next step is how it feels in the hallway of life. I needed God's light to give me direction, but all I heard was *wait.* So I stood in the dark and anxiously waited.

Why did I have to wait? I felt I needed to know what was next. I recalled the pastor saying, "You're about to turn the corner and blessings await."

My mind assumed Jesus would perform a miracle and give us funding for the building. I'd rather receive the miracle than have my heart crushed. I wanted to inherit the blessings Jesus had promised. I wished for many things: a paid-for building, debt-free clinic, people to minister to, and paid positions.

A few nights after I'd received the word about the "hallway," I had a dream. Jimmy, our son Mason, and I were heading to a beautiful hotel room. I knew our destination, I just didn't know how we were getting there.

As we left our house, we walked down the streets of a city. Jimmy stopped and pointed to a sewer drain, saying, "Here's how we're supposed to get there."

I looked at him in disgust. "I'm not going through the sewer drains to get to our hotel. No way!"

Jimmy proceeded to pull off the sewer drain and Mason jumped right down. Jimmy followed behind. He reached his hand out and said, "Are you coming?"

I stood there angry. Again he said, "Are you coming?"

Though frustrated, I said, "Fine!" Jimmy helped me down into the sewer, and we headed to our beautiful hotel room through a yucky and smelly underground drain. As we walked through the sewer, the water became shallower and soon disappeared. I realized we were on a bright red brick road. In the distance, I could hear vehicles and other voices. As we continued to walk, we came upon a beautiful underground city.

I became amazed, "I can't believe this! Nobody knows this place exists. There's an entire underground city that's flourishing, and it's beautiful." I wanted to explore the city, but Jimmy said we had to keep moving.

We ventured through the city and came to an elevator. We rode up to our hotel, which was above ground. As we traveled up the elevator, my mind continued to be amazed. I couldn't believe there was an underground city. It was a secret very few people knew about. In my dream, I heard the Lord say, *Very few people will ever see the underground city, because they aren't willing to go through the sewers to get to their next stop.*

We arrived and found we were too early to check in. I told Jimmy I'd ask and see if by chance, our room was ready. I approached the hotel desk to ask about early check-in and the lady replied, "You're room isn't ready yet, but if you want a different room we can check you in now." Seeing my hesitation, she then said, "I can show you the other room, then you can decide."

I said, "Okay, we'll look at it."

As we approached the alternate room, I caught a glimpse of another room, to the right. The door stood open and maids were inside cleaning. The chambers appeared immaculate. Windows covered two walls, stretching from floor to ceiling. It had an amazing view of the beach and ocean.

Without being told, I knew it was the room we'd initially reserved. We looked at the other room, but my heart desired the one with the beautiful windows and view. I thanked the lady for showing us the second room, but we'd decided to wait for our original reservation.

She said, "Okay, actually your room is across the hall." As she pointed to the room I saw first, and said, "You can wait in the hallway if you want. It appears the maids are almost finished cleaning. Once they're done, you're more than welcome to go in. It'll take about ten minutes."

I replied, "That'd be great, thanks."

Jimmy, Mason, and I were waiting in the hallway ... then I woke up. I sat up in bed wishing I'd slept long enough to know what happened next. I lay back down and tried forcing myself to go back to sleep, but I couldn't.

I said, "Lord, really, the hallway? Can I ever get out of this place? How long do I have to wait?"

Jesus didn't answer.

One week before our building deadline approached, my step-dad, who manages business office rentals, told me he had a building we could use. His current renter wanted to relocate and this particular building would be available. We wouldn't have to sign a contract and we could use it as long as we needed.

I told him, "Thanks, but first we'll see what the Lord does." My heart had been set on the first building. To my dismay, our deadline came and we didn't have the money to purchase the building. To make matters worse, we lost our deposit.

Inside I was crushed, and at the same time, furious. The Lord had said to step out in faith. Our team did so, in obedience, and I felt He didn't show up. What would people think of me? Did I fail somehow? I must not have heard the voice of the Lord correctly.

I cried out in anger, "Where were you? Why'd you tell us to move in faith if you were going to leave us hang out to dry?"

This pierced my heart. It brought up old wounds of rejection, being forgotten, and given empty promises. I knew that wasn't the Lord's character, but what was He doing?

The next day I told my step-dad we'd love to use his building. We then applied for small community grants to purchase the supplies needed to open the clinic.

The next few months I continued reading my Bible and attending church, but my relationship with God had changed. It felt distant. I felt betrayed. Even though I knew it wasn't true, I questioned Jesus's love for me.

In time, I began letting Jesus back into my wounded heart. My anger faded, but I had yet to face my pain. Finally, the time came when I could ask, "What happened? Where were you? Did I hear you wrong? Why did you allow me to walk through this painful experience?"

Jesus said, *Write down the promises I've given you.*

I then wrote down the promises He had given for my life as well as the clinic. He then said, *Yes, I've promised these things, but did I give you a timeline? I told you to go after the building, but I didn't tell you that you'd get it now. The way I'm going to establish this clinic is like going through the sewers. This clinic will be established like nothing has ever been established before. People won't question how it happened, they'll know it was me."*

After hearing His words, my heart recalled the dream about the sewers and the hallway. To get to our hotel, we needed to travel through the sewers. Our room hadn't been ready. But, we willingly waited in the hallway for our reserved room. We didn't settle. We awaited the promise.

I felt like an idiot. I'd raced ahead of the Lord. In my mind, when He told us to go after the building, I assumed it meant that *particular* building would be ours, *right now*. I learned the hard way not to assume anything.

I asked, "Were we not supposed to go after the building?"

He replied, *You've done as I've asked, you heard me right. That was your faith deposit.*

"Why didn't you tell me we wouldn't immediately get it?"

Would you have still put yourself out there and gone after it?

My heart sunk and I said, "No. I would've said, 'just tell me when it's time for us to get a building, then we'll step out in faith.'"

The Lord said, *Trust me, this is for your protection.*

I mentally rolled my eyes, thinking, "Okay, whatever you say."

This was a painful time. Through this process, the Holy Spirit walked me straight into humility. I could hear the voice of the Lord, but realized He would be the one to establish the clinic, not me.

Humility taught me it's God's grace that allows me to hear his voice. Not by my works, but by his love and tender mercies alone.

In hindsight, I realized pride had hidden itself in my heart. People saw me as laid back and humble. I knew the right actions and words, but was blind to my places of self-righteousness. Now, I'm grateful Jesus had enough love and grace to expose the darkness. I desired a pure heart. But, to receive it, I had to go through His refining fire.

I'm thankful the clinic didn't take off as fast as I'd planned. There were many lessons I needed to learn. The most important was glorifying Jesus above everything and giving Him all the credit.

If the clinic would've succeeded through my efforts, I admit I would've been prideful. I would've felt blessed and favored. Thankfully, the Lord took care of my ego and taught me humility. He showed me He deserves the glory, not me. If I do something to gain attention for myself, my motives are wrong. I understood that concept. But, when ambushed by pride you become so blinded you don't realize you're operating in it. The Holy Spirit taught me to be clothed in humility and keep a posture of submission. This life is about God bringing restoration to His people. I'm just a vessel.

The journey of securing a building for the clinic has been like walking through sewers. Stay hopeful and know it's okay to have messy and ugly stuff come up in your heart. That's what we want, because when we see it, the Lord's going to take care of it! He wants every part of us, even if it's not the cleanest or most pure area. Jesus makes our heart pure. In our weakest and messiest areas is where God produces the most fruit.

Life is a journey of being transformed into the image of Christ. I'm not fully transformed, but a work in progress. He's answering my prayers of obtaining an authentic and transparent heart. Through seasons of finding a venue for the clinic, I received the next clue in my treasure hunt. *"I'm in process and that's okay".* My self-righteous and perfectionist attitudes had to go. As long as I walk with Jesus, my process is good and I can't mess it up.

Lord, we open our hearts to you, no matter how ugly and messy they may appear. We will submit to your ways as you take us through your refining fire. I pray for an enriching of the soil in our hearts so the seeds you plant will take root and grow into something beautiful. Please give us grace as we walk through our process with you. Thanks for seeing us as worthy and taking us on a journey of transforming us into

your image!

Blessings,

Kara☺

Giants

As we continue along the path of our destiny and walk through spiritual seasons, we'll encounter giants. Giants are things in life that try to distract us, make us stop, or cause us to veer away from walking our destiny. We all face giants. Some are easier to face than others, but they attack our weakest flaws. Giants are different for each person. A few examples are fear, jealousy, hatred, control, passivity, people pleasing, addictions, lust, or unforgiveness.

My biggest giant is fear. I've struggled with fear since I was a child. It's a family trait and had been instilled in me at a young age. Fear of the Lord and common sense dangers are *healthy* fears. Common sense teaches us to be aware of our surroundings. Fear of the Lord, helps us develop a deep reverence for the things of God. *Unhealthy fears* make us stop dead in our tracks. Fear makes me feel like shrinking back into a corner and curling up in a ball. Be attentive to what's going on around you, but don't let fear keep you from doing things you enjoy, or what Jesus calls you to do.

Fearful thoughts used to torment my mind. I initially *recognized* fear as one of my giants when I first walked with Jesus. The Lord taught me to stand toe to toe with the different aspects of fear. As I stood and faced each giant, He showed up, bringing deliverance and healing.

I love music and worship. I'd often put on headphones, sit on my living room floor, and spend time with the Lord. One day, I was kneeling with my head on the floor. I tried to enter a quiet time of prayer. Sometimes entering that space was hard. Thoughts would race through my mind and I couldn't shut it off. I'd find myself shuffling schedules and tasks for the day and upcoming week. When it came to spending time with Jesus, my mind would be my worst enemy. I'd pray and push for that place until my mind cleared and nothing mattered, but that moment with Jesus. I'd then get lost in the music.

As I lay there, scrunched forward, fear began to torment me. It said, "You better look around and make sure no one's breaking into your house. Someone may come in and stab you in the back, then you'd be dead. Hurry, look around!"

I knew it seemed crazy, but I heard the thoughts and felt the uneasiness throughout my body. It kept trying to distract me. I had to pray against it. I said, "Fear, you have no place in this house, and you have no place in me. Jesus didn't give me a spirit of fear and timidity, but a Spirit of power, love, peace, and a sound mind."

I had to stay in the place of prayer, keep my eyes closed, and not look around. I wasn't going to open my eyes and give in to fear. After a few minutes of continuous prayer, I felt the Holy Spirit. The initial feeling of uneasiness left. A sense of peace, stillness, and a clear mind overcame me. I entered that sacred space and it felt as if time stood still.

When we feel a giant trying to wage war with us, we feel negative emotions. They vary for each individual and situation. A few examples of negative emotions are insecurity, fear, hate, bitterness, doubt, unbelief, jealousy, inadequacy, selfishness, and unworthiness. None of these are our inheritance from the Lord. We must hold our stance against them and seek the Lord in prayer.

Don't give in to the giant! When we ask, Jesus will come to our rescue. He comes and claims victory for us. He'll remove the giant from our space. Once the atmosphere is clear, you'll feel safe, peace, rest, loved, and calm. Then you'll see the giant is about the size of an ant. It's never as big as it initially appears. Giants in your life will come and go. I've faced many different "fear" giants, but my first step was to recognize them. Then, I'd pray the truth and promises of God until I felt His presence.

My largest war with fear occurred the summer of 2013. For four years I'd told Jesus, "Send me and my family to be

missionaries. We'll go wherever you want. Just not to Africa."
I'm half Hispanic, and I know a little Spanish. I know enough to
understand the basics, as long as they're spoken slowly. I didn't
know anything about Africans. I was clueless about their
culture, language, differing religions, and lifestyles. I wanted to
do mission work where it felt familiar.

For three months, I talked to people who randomly spoke
about Africa. Finally, I said, "Okay Lord, you have my attention.
What are you saying, and why is everything I'm hearing,
highlighting Africa?"

I'm calling you to Africa soon, will you go?

My fears of walking into the unknown resurfaced. I
mentally nodded *no*, coming up with every excuse why I didn't
need to go to Africa.

"Everybody goes to Africa! I want to go somewhere that's
not over populated with missionaries. Take me to a Spanish
speaking country, where I like the food, and know a little of the
culture."

Again Jesus said, *I'm calling you to Africa, will you go?*

Sighing deeply I said, "Yea, I'll go, but with whom?" He
didn't answer me. Over the next couple weeks I had to convince
myself I'd be going to Africa. I prayed for the Lord to give me a
heart for Africa. Over the course of a couple months, I traveled
to different churches to hear speakers, and everyone had a
missionary from Africa. My heart shifted. The speakers were

genuine and loving. My heart fell in love with the character of the African people. I wanted to learn about their life and culture. My spirit was ready to go.

Two weeks later, I received a phone call from a lady I used to work with. I hadn't seen her for three years. She said she was going to Africa to serve and share the gospel in three months, and wanted a travel partner. She and her husband had been there two years ago and she wanted to go back. She asked me to go with her.

Feeling numb, I said, "Let me pray about it and I'll let you know in a couple weeks."

I sat down and tried recalling everything that had recently happened. Jesus said I'd be going to Africa soon. But I questioned if this was the "soon" He was talking about. It'd just be the two of us and we'd be working with a local pastor. I knew her, but not intimately. Could I travel half way around the world with someone I didn't know well? This sounded crazy. I didn't know if I was ready to go. It couldn't be this soon. I'd miss my husband and kids. I wanted to pretend this opportunity hadn't come up. I ignored it for the next two weeks.

Eventually, I knew I had to let her know if I'd go or not. Finally, I asked Jesus, "Am I supposed to travel with her to Africa?"

He replied, *Go, the road is paved.* Jesus reminded me of scriptures I'd been reading that confirmed my calling. I talked to my husband and he said, "Go. If the Lord's telling you to go, you need to go."

I told the lady I'd go. We started talking more on the phone, meeting, and planning with the pastor in Africa about how we'd spend our time. I became excited. I told my parents and grandparents. They were very hesitant and I didn't initially receive their blessing. But my husband encouraged me to be obedient to the Lord.

Throughout the next three months, my fears became tangible. I feared straining my relationship with my extended family. I feared I wouldn't receive funding. I feared the plane would crash. I feared I wouldn't make it back home to see my husband and kids again. These fears might seem silly to some, but for me, they cut deep. Many different fears were my giants.

In the end, the Spirit of the Lord changed my family's heart. They released me to Jesus and His will. I knew they were nervous, but I now had their blessing. I received all my funding and I was ready to go. A few weeks before our flight, terrorists attacked the country we would be traveling to. High alerts were issued, warning people not to travel to this specific country. The embassy shut down. I'm not one to watch the news, but people were quick to inform me of the warnings. I know they told me because they cared, but it made my fears escalate. I questioned if I was supposed to go. I sought the Lord in prayer and He continued telling me to go.

One week before we left for Africa, news agencies reported that the airport we were flying into had caught on fire. I again questioned my upcoming travels and asked Jesus, "Am I supposed to go or not? I need to know. I want to come home to my family. I need you to settle my spirit."

He said, *Kara, what keeps you from going? If I told you that you'll travel to Africa, have a great time, and come home with no problems would you go?*

I replied, "Yes. I want to go, but I fear for my life and safety."

Is fear from me?

Peace settled over me and my mind became still. "No," I said.

Is fear the only thing keeping you from going?

I looked at my heart and my desire was to go. Only one thing would keep me home. "Yeah, fear is the only reason I'd not want to go. Will I come home to my family?"

I could feel His smile. *Yes, you're coming home. You haven't done what you were created to do. I'll bring you home to your family.*

"Alright," I said. "Let's do it."

The morning came to leave. Though determined, I still felt weepy, knowing I'd miss my family. Our flights were great, but I still heard a faint whisper of fear. I continued to stay grounded in prayer, read my Bible, and focused on Jesus, not the *"what if's."* By the third day, I felt better, and my heart began to open to those beautiful people.

They loved me as if I were their own. They lived in mud huts with dirt floors and ate one meal a day, but they were sincere and genuine people.

The pastor we worked with had many different outreaches. We met with widow groups, traveled to HIV/AIDS clinics, and visited different churches. Each group had different projects they were working on for their community. It's a beautiful concept and how they truly lived in fellowship. It wasn't what anyone could get for themselves, but how to work together to make their communities thrive.

One night, I lay in bed with my headphones on. My heart was open, but broken at the same time. I felt deeply for these people. How could I help them? What was my mission here? They struggled to meet daily needs. The government overlooked their poverty and seemed unwilling to provide for them. Left to fend for themselves, their daily focus was *survival.*

In this new pain, I asked Jesus, "What's different about this place than my other mission trips?"

He replied, *When you leave nobody's coming.*

"What do you mean?" I asked.

On every other mission trip, there's been teams coming and going. But when you leave this time, there won't be anyone coming. They'll be waiting for you to return.

My heart broke even more as I recalled my previous argument that Africa had too many missionaries. Well, this place had no American missionaries.

I said, "What am I supposed to do? I'm only one person?"

Jesus said, *Finish school and you'll come to establish a clinic. You'll teach the locals how to run it and you can bring teams over from the States to serve.*

My heart leapt with joy. I received the next piece of my treasure hunt. ***"I will be part of overseas missions."*** This didn't necessarily mean I'd live there, but I began to recall my past mission experiences.

After starting school, and three years lapsing between mission trips, I'd put mission work on the back burner. I realized my previous trips were seasons for learning my destiny and discovering my identity in Christ. I had convinced myself I'd be okay if I wasn't an overseas missionary. Now, after my time in Africa, the burning desire for mission work ignited once again in my heart. This time it felt different.

I had already known I was supposed to open a clinic at home. But now, I saw the connection with mission work. I used to believe it was stay home or go, but God is preparing a way for me to do both. The clinic will be established in my hometown, but we'll run mission teams around the world. Starting in Africa.

I was beginning to put together some of the puzzle pieces I had gathered the past eight years. I'm so thankful I faced my fears and traveled to Africa. This new vision became the driving force to finish my FNP. I had two years of school left, but my hope and joy were restored.

Jesus has indeed, delivered me from fear. But sometimes, I still see it rear its ugly head. I'm so grateful, because recognition comes more quickly and I can call it out. I refuse to be trapped under the control of a giant. I pray until I feel God's peace, stillness, and love.

Facing giants can be painful, scary, and at times frustrating. It may expose old wounds. But Jesus is there, waiting to overcome it and bring healing. Know you're not alone. Everyone has giants. Giants attack our weaknesses and their intensity increases when we're at our lowest point. Thankfully, we have a Savior who stands and fights for us.

It never fails. Every time the Holy Spirit moves and places the next step, the giants rise up. They'll try bringing fear, discouragement, doubt, and unbelief. They tried to steal my hope and trust in the Lord. The giants tried to keep me from traveling to Africa. It was there I received the next piece of my treasure hunt. They wanted to block and distort my vision and make me veer off the path of my destiny. They tormented my mind with lies. I had to choose to hold tight to the promises from Jesus. Know your promises. Write them down. Declare them over yourself, even when it appears far from reach. Speak those promises over you and your family. They are your inheritance and blessings from the Lord. He will bring them to fruition.

The clinic isn't running mission teams yet. We've been through seasons of establishing our foundation. Currently, we're entering a season of expanding, while putting into place programs and outreaches. Although we aren't going to Africa right now, or next month, I hang on to the promise we will. I continue to talk about it when casting vision for the clinic. Sometime in our future, we will run mission teams around the world. We'll provide medical care, letting people know they're seen, valued, worthy, and loved.

Lord, thank you for being the deliverer and healer of our heart. I pray for strength, wisdom, and confidence for us to face our giants. I pray you will teach us to recognize our giant and call it out. Expose the lies from the enemy that try to hinder us from moving forward along the path of our destiny. Thank you for having our backs and overcoming for us. You are our victor and to you we give all the praise, honor, and glory!

Blessings,

Kara☺

Breathe

Have you ever been outside in the wintertime, when you want to hold your breath because it's too cold to inhale? The bitter air freezes your mouth and throat, leaving them dry and numb. Every breath feels shorter and shallower. You start to shiver. Maybe your mind begins to panic or your heart races. You try pulling your scarf or collar above your nose, but it doesn't keep you from wishing for a place of warmth. You long for hot chocolate, fuzzy socks, and a blanket. Eventually you spot shelter and make a dash for it.

We all have places that make us feel cozy and safe. It could be a coffee shop, a warm car, or your own house. As you enter your safe haven, you may rub your hands or stand next to a fire. Soon, the shivering ceases and you're able to take deeper breaths. The heat is calming. Your heart has slowed. Your mind stills. You feel relaxed, comfortable, and at peace.

One day, I was at gymnastics watching my kids practice. I was surrounded by noise and chaos. Three ladies to my right were loud and giggling. The gentleman to my left talked business on his cell phone. Parents in front looked tired and exhausted. They were trying to make their two young children sit still and be quiet. As a mother of three, I remembered those days. Knowing it's normal for toddlers to be rambunctious, into everything, and testing your patience.

As I sat on the bleachers, irritation bubbled inside me. The feeling of being trapped in a cold draft arose and I longed to escape the noise. I felt distress, similar to winter air stealing my breath. My heart raced, my breathing became shallow, and my upper body tensed. I wanted to sit peacefully and watch my kids perform. I desired rest, quiet, and stillness. I wanted to tune out the commotion.

I leaned against the wall and closed my eyes. My heart looked to the Lord and I said, "Are you there? Please still my heart and mind because I'm about to explode." I could feel the familiar panic closing in on me.

I longed for a warm fire. I concentrated on taking slow, deep, breaths. I told myself to be calm. I started to zone out. All the noise and chaos around me began to fade. I entered a different reality. Although the pulse of everyday life surrounded me, I felt at peace and relaxed. My frustration dissipated.

I opened my eyes and I watched my kids, but my ears were closed. I realized the noise and chaos resembled distractions from everyday life. We can choose to join the commotion or live with peace.

Life on earth is beautiful, but it can also be crazy busy. The enemy wants us to pack our schedules, keeping our minds focused on the next task or agenda item. He doesn't want you to have time to connect with Jesus. If we're not careful, our schedules will consume and drain us. We end up running on empty. And the people who suffer most are those closest to us.

At one point, my calendar became out of control. My husband would comment about it, but I kept pushing forward. I didn't realize I was teaching our children to be equally busy. I thought my life should be all about productivity, but later realized what I needed more was space to *breathe*. This was a life lesson I learned and hold close to my heart.

God created me to be mission focused and goal driven. I like being productive and completing tasks. Once I reach a set of goals, I make new ones, and start moving towards *accomplishment*. It makes me feel like I'm being helpful and using my time wisely. I want to be a good steward of money, education, and resources. This is a great gift, but when not kept in balance, creates stress and self-glorification. When unbalanced, this lifestyle keeps me in perpetual motion, never allowing me time to rest.

While working on my FNP degree, I had weeks planned out in advance. I juggled work, school, clinical time, kids, recreational sports activities, and family. I'm great at multitasking. The problem is, my plans rarely panned out. The Lord always had a better idea. Four difficult years of graduate school became my training ground to learn balance.

I first experienced insight with balancing my schedule when pregnant with our youngest daughter. It was November and I was in my first semester of graduate school. I'd put in my two-week notice at the office in which I worked, as I was taking a new position at the local hospital. The hospital was short staffed and needed me to start immediately. There were three weeks my two jobs overlapped, but I wanted extra money for Christmas. So, I decided to push through.

About one week into working both jobs, I fell ill. My symptoms included congested sinuses, plugged ears, and a cough. With two weeks to go, I convinced myself I could do this. I'm strong and healthy. I could keep pushing through. A few days later, I became weak and listless. It felt as if I were sleepwalking as I checked off each completed task.

One evening I began having trouble breathing. I found it difficult to take deep breaths. I took a shower, which helped, but I felt drained and exhausted. During the night I developed chills and night sweats. I went to work the next morning, but was sent home. This forced me to go to the doctor. I received a prescription for an upper respiratory infection and strep throat. For the next three days, I lay on the couch, unable to work or go to school. All this happened because I didn't know how to say 'no' and make time to rest.

Being couch bound and feeling weak, I inquired of the Lord. "What's going on? I never get sick. I have a full schedule and I wanted extra money for Christmas."

Jesus said, *Life is about balance. Sometimes you'll run and sometimes you'll rest. It's important to learn the difference. You need to listen to your body and rest when it's time to rest.*

I replied, "How do I know?"

I'm teaching you.

I've had many opportunities to learn about balance. Each time, I listened to the cues a little sooner because I didn't want to get sick or waste time on the couch. About a year later, I received another revelation about schedules. I have issues with control. It took many lessons to loosen my grip on it. I'm still learning, but with every new insight, I receive more and more freedom.

It was a Monday night. I put our kids to bed and I sat down to type a research paper. I had my schedule planned out for the next ten days. In addition to my research paper, I had discussion board posts to complete and a test to study for. I'd committed to volunteer for a friend's ministry and I'd been scheduled to work two, twelve-hour shifts at the hospital. My 'to do' list was written down to the hour. At first, it started out great and I was doing well. By Thursday, I was going into work drained. It would be a long twelve hours.

On my way to work I prayed, "Lord, please give me the energy and the grace to do my work today. Help me to love my patients like you do." Despite my prayer, work was draining. I barely had time to eat lunch. I returned home to prepare dinner, help with homework, pack lunches, give baths, and put kids to bed. Although I had help from my husband, I was exhausted. I wanted to go to bed, but had to stick to my schedule and research my discussion board posts. My schedule didn't allow me time to take a break.

I sat on the couch with my laptop, fighting to keep my eyes open. I kept talking to myself, saying, "Focus! Stay awake and finish this." It was impossible and I kept falling asleep. Each time my head fell against the cushions, I'd jerk myself upright, pushing myself until I finished my work. I had to stick to my plan because I had an agenda. Unfortunately, that forced me to work until one a.m.

I had to get up in five and a half hours to get my kids ready for school, and I had clinical rotation the next morning. That isn't enough sleep for me. I'm a person who needs eight hours of rest. When sleep deprived, my mind becomes fogged and I'm a grouch.

The next morning I could barely get out of bed. I felt as if my cover of grace had left me. My devotion and prayer time became a habit of indifference. I'd talk, but not be engaged in conversation. I went through the motions, but my mind and heart weren't present. All I thought about was checking items off my list and when I could go back to bed. I stupidly prayed for the energy and ability to stick to my planned schedule.

That Friday night, I sat on the couch and fell asleep while typing on my laptop. I woke up at two a.m. and realized I'd made no progress. I grew frustrated because I didn't stick to my plan. Now, I wouldn't have time to finish all my work. When would I ever complete my to-do-list?

I became irritated with the Lord. "I prayed for grace. Why didn't you keep me awake to finish my paper? You know I have a schedule and my time's limited. *You're* the one who told me to go back to school. Why aren't you helping me? I need this paper done so I can study for my test this weekend."

Instead of answering, the Lord said, *Go to bed*.

"What?"

Again I heard the same response, *Go to bed*.

I didn't ask again. I marched myself to our bedroom and collapsed.

I slept until ten a.m. and woke feeling refreshed. I savored the breakfast I ate with my family. For thirty minutes, I felt as if I could inhale and exhale fully. The demands of my self-imposed agenda no longer suffocated me.

I finished all my assignments, studied for my test, and took pleasure in family time. It's amazing how the Lord's plan and His schedule freed me from my stress. How does He do that? It didn't make sense, but I accomplished everything that needed to be done. Most of all, I enjoyed the weekend!

The following Monday, I sat down to talk with Jesus. I sat in our recliner with my Bible and Chai Tea. Sipping on my tea, I closed my eyes and began praying.

I said, "Lord, I can't keep living like this. I'm overwhelmed by the demands of life. Eventually, I feel weak and my mind gets fogged. I want my family to have the best of me, not my leftovers. I need to know the secret to my schedule."

Jesus replied, *Yes, you're right, your life is busy, but you're doing things that aren't on your plate for this season. You're in charge of your schedule. What do you want?*

My heart cried out, "I want you! I want to be in alignment with you in each season of my life. Show me what to cut out and what to invest in. I need you to control my schedule."

That day, I surrendered my plans and habit of multitasking to the Lord. He showed me how to live with a Kingdom agenda. Jesus also explained balance and seasons of activities.

Each activity represents a portion of food on your plate. Each season, our involvement and what we're to focus on changes. Sometimes, we'll be led to cut things we considered good. Like switching out steak for chicken, or cutting the green bean portion in half to make room for a different vegetable.

We may be involved in church activities or Bible studies that are life giving, but it's important to be obedient and shift with the seasons. It's hard to stop being involved in something we know to be good. Remember, just because we step down or stop an activity, doesn't mean we don't believe in its importance. The Lord will shift our portions, and that's okay. As we step down, it gives someone else an opportunity to become involved while we move to the next season.

When the Lord rearranges our plate or shifts our responsibilities, we have three choices. We can push through, trying to manage the status quo ourselves. We can create our own path. Or, we can submit to the shift. If we choose to push through or create our own path, our lives become stressful, chaotic, and off balance. Veering off our path puts our hearts at risk for self-righteousness, pride, and selfish ambition. We become dependent on our own abilities and not His. Sometimes, choosing wrong paths creates the toughest lessons. I recommend we submit to the shift.

I've always had a difficult time changing my seasons. Managing graduate school, church, family, sports activities, and work became four years of learning. Now, I know when a shift is coming, but that doesn't make it easy. I've learned to draw close to the Lord, seeking clarity and direction in my personal walk.

I've been involved in ministries, Bible studies, small groups, house churches, and worship/prayer nights. The Lord has led me in and out of each one. When it's time to shift, He won't give us the grace to continue carrying work from previous commitments. Grace covers the current season and arrangement on our plates.

While in school, I couldn't wait to be finished. I thought my schedule would ease up and I'd have free time. Once I graduated, my free time quickly filled with volunteering, work, and the clinic. There've been times I felt *the winter air* taking my breath away, causing panic. Yet, I've learned to stop and evaluate the portions on my plate. I've learned when to move and when to rest.

Whenever I feel stressed about life, I find my agenda has filled itself up again. I'll then stop, look at my schedule, and start removing things. Sometimes I'll have to call and change appointments, or cancel an event we'd originally planned to attend.

I've learned I can't please everybody. I continue learning how to say 'no' to events, plans, and phone calls. I choose to make space in my life for God, Jimmy, my kids, and myself. Those are the people who deserve my whole heart and attention.

One fall morning, I was walking a trail in a nearby woods. It was beautiful outside, mid sixties, with a cool autumn breeze. As I walked, I felt happy I had space to do something I enjoyed. I took deep breaths of crisp air. It smelled fresh. It felt cool in my throat. My spirit and lungs felt relaxed and purified.

For an instant, my mind rushed through everything I had to do: laundry, dishes, groceries, balance the checkbook, pay bills, and clean the house. In that moment, I said 'no' to the chores of life. My to-do list could wait. That day I decided to walk, let my mind be still, enjoy the moment, and *breathe*.

As you walk the path of your destiny, the bitter cold will try to freeze you, making your mind and heart numb. The busyness of life keeps you from having time to invest in your relationship with Jesus, your family, and friends.

As followers of Jesus, we have the choice to let the cold steal our breath away, or say 'no' to the demands of life. The best choice is to find a nice cozy place to rest and breathe. We are in charge of our schedules. We don't have to submit to the chaos life throws at us. I choose to live a life of freedom, love, joy, peace, and stillness. I choose to balance my schedule and ***"Create Space to Breathe."***

Lord, settle in our spirit to know it's healthy to take space for ourselves. Reveal to us the portions on our plates this season. May we find freedom in saying "no" and know it's okay. I pray we'd be intentional to create space to enjoy life, soak in your presence, and breathe.

Blessings,

Kara☺

Jump

Walking the path of our destiny is an exciting and adventurous journey. We enter and leave various seasons. It's crucial we walk with Jesus and know there are times to walk, run, or rest. These seasons prepare us for the path ahead; because as we venture along our journey, we encounter obstacles. Yes, Jesus is with us, and He's capable of removing hardships. But sometimes, we approach a cliff edge and the only way to cross is to jump!

Can you image walking up to the edge of a cliff, knowing you have to cross over? There's no other option, but to jump. I would always panic. I'd think of every excuse to take a different route. Jumping requires we use our faith muscles. One day, I asked the Lord, "What does child-like faith look like?" He reminded me of a situation when our son was two years old.

Our son is fearless, fun-loving, and determined. We were both in my bedroom while I put away laundry. He'd climbed on top of our bed, which sat high due to a thick mattress and box springs. I turned my back to hang clothes in my closet. I could hear him jumping on the bed and babbling. I turned to grab more clothes and I saw our son mid air, leaping for me. There was no way he could've jumped all the way to me, but he didn't care. He knew I was standing there, he trusted me, and he had faith I'd catch him. I lunged forward, dropped to my knees, and thankfully caught him. Recalling that moment, I heard the Lord say, *That's what child-like faith looks like.*

Faith is a spiritual muscle that needs exercised. Imagine going to a gym and working out. When you begin bench-pressing, you don't put hundreds of pounds on the bar. Most likely, you'll start out small and light. First, you bench-press the bar without extra weight. Over time, you'll increase the amount of weight. We all must start somewhere. And, it should always be in the small beginnings.

As I reflect over the past ten years, I've seen the Lord ask me to step out in faith, starting with small steps. I began jumping from rock to rock. Over time, I've learned to jump cliff edge to cliff edge.

I initially started exercising my faith while learning to hear God's voice. I wanted to be a vessel for the Lord. I hungered to inspire people to be who God created them to be. I desired to call out treasures in people's hearts they couldn't see. I prayed for prophetic words and scriptures to share with people, to encourage them.

After a few months, the Lord answered my prayers. One time, while in quiet time with the Lord, I envisioned a picture of a gentleman. God didn't give me a word, scripture, or further direction. I only saw the man. I asked Jesus, "When am I going to see this man and what am I supposed to tell him?" I received no answer.

Two days later my family and I were getting ready for church. I had worship music playing and suddenly my stomach began turning in knots. I felt really nervous, but had no idea why.

I said, "Lord, what's going on?"

He didn't reply. I had an impression the Holy Spirit would move that day at church. The uncertainty and lack of direction made me feel squeamish. As we headed to church, I told my husband, "The Lord's going to do something today, but I have no idea what He's going to ask of me."

We arrived and took the kids to class before entering the sanctuary. During worship, a specific scripture popped into my head. I grabbed my Bible and looked it up. It wasn't a nice, mushy, gushy verse. It was a scripture that spoke a harsh truth. I suddenly felt nauseated.

"Lord, what am I supposed to do with this?" He didn't answer with words, but reminded me of the vision I had of a man.

I thought, "What did I get myself into? Why did I ask the Lord to use me? I'm not confident enough to do this."

I sighed deeply, and agreed to do it. "Okay, Lord you have to give me faith and courage. Besides, how am I supposed to say the scripture? It's not a 'feel good' word."

He said, *Sit and wait.* I felt peace overcome me. My nausea subsided and the knots in my stomach released. I sat down beside my husband and listened to the service.

During the sermon, the pastor mentioned a few concepts that confirmed the word I was supposed to tell this man. I still didn't know whom or where this gentleman was located.

Towards the end of the message, the knots and nausea returned. I looked around the sanctuary to see if I saw someone who represented the man in my vision. I'd look at someone and say to the Lord, "Is that him?" I never heard yes or no, but felt discernment in my spirit. When I looked at people, I listened to the Holy Spirit and waited for an answer. If it weren't the right person, I'd feel a peace come over me, with a feeling to keep looking.

Eventually, I saw a younger man and my nervous system heightened. Although I was sure this was the man, I tested it. I looked at someone else and asked, "Maybe it's him?" As I looked at someone else, all my symptoms subsided. Then I looked back at the young gentleman and they returned.

I knew this was the guy. But what was I supposed to tell him? I needed the word.

I asked Jesus, "What am I supposed to say besides this scripture? You speak truth, but it's always released in love. This scripture isn't very loving."

Jesus replied, *Go over introduce yourself and start talking.*

I panicked, "I need to know what to say. When am I supposed to go over there? The preacher is still talking!"

You'll know.

I got flustered. I had no specifics besides a man, and a harsh bible verse. My flesh wanted to say 'forget it, I don't want to be used.' Yet, my spirit desired to see God move in my life. I knew I had to jump. I was willing to risk my ego and face my fears of uncertainty. But, I still had to convince myself to do it.

I told myself, "What's the worse he could say, you're crazy and you have no idea what you're talking about?" I'd either make a fool of myself or watch God show up.

A song played at the end of the service. A few seconds in, I felt a gentle spiritual nudge. It was time to release the word to this man. I took a deep breath and moved my feet. I approached the gentleman, stuck out my hand to shake his, and introduced myself.

I started the conversation, "S-S-Sir, it's a pleasure to meet you. Do you mind if I encourage you for a minute?"

He nodded.

I said, "During worship the Lord put you on my heart…." My heart, spirit, and the Holy Spirit became one. The rest of the conversation I cannot recall, for the Spirit spoke through me. As I prayed for him, he broke down in tears. The Lord showed up and encountered him. I was ecstatic. I saw the Lord move! He encountered us both. He used me and I felt honored. Although the verse was harsh, Holy Spirit had seasoned it with love.

This was my first encounter with the Lord using me to give a prophetic word. Along the path of my destiny I've had many more opportunities. I started with small steps, and the distance between them slowly increased. Using faith muscles is something the Lord establishes within you, and will continue to strengthen. There have been times I've jumped and my foot slipped, but Jesus was always there to help me up and give me another chance. If I missed or messed up, He'd cover me in grace.

Another day, I knew I had a word for a lady. I didn't know her personally, but I'd seen her before. Again, it wasn't a 'feel good' word. It was a word about past pain and wounds that Jesus wanted to bring healing to.

These words are difficult for me because I hear the giant voices of fear, doubt, and unbelief. They torment my mind, saying, "You're crazy! What if she doesn't have any past pain? You don't know for sure." The giants always throw out the 'what if's.' I have to pray against it and trust the Lord. It's one of many aspects of strengthening my faith muscles.

At church, I viewed this particular lady from a distance. This time, I knew the word I was supposed to share. I told the Lord, "If you want me to talk to her, bring us together in passing after church."

After the service, my husband and I headed out of the sanctuary. I saw her standing off to the side with her family. The giant of fear held me captive. I walked past her, making excuses why I shouldn't stop and talk with her.

The church we attended didn't teach or talk about the prophetic, and I feared she'd think I was crazy. Jimmy and I gathered our children and walked to the car. As I closed the car door, my heart sank. I was ashamed. I felt like I'd missed my chance. I apologized to the Lord that I didn't trust Him and had given in to fear. Sitting in my humiliation, I thought Jesus wouldn't want to use me anymore because I wasn't obedient. Internally, I beat myself up. I told myself I was stupid, a failure, and unworthy. I looked to Jesus and said, "I'm sorry, I missed my chance. I can't believe I didn't walk over and say hello. I understand if you don't want to use me anymore." I felt his love embrace me.

You didn't miss it.

I replied, "Yeah, I did. You set the stage and I walked past her without saying a single word. Now I'm going home."

Trust me, you'll have another chance.

The next Sunday, I was confident and ready to release the word. The Lord had prepared me and had given me courage. My husband and I sat down, I looked around, but she was nowhere to be found. In the middle of worship, she entered the sanctuary and sat right in front of my husband and me. The Lord had set the stage, giving me a second chance. I was ready. I felt confident and bold.

After church, I walked towards her while the giants again told me lies. This time, I felt grounded in my assignment from Jesus. Despite my fear and unbelief, I approached her, reached out my hand, and introduced myself. I had to stand toe-to-toe with my fears and do it, even though I felt afraid. I shared the word and prayed with her. She thanked me and we were both on our way.

Walking out to my vehicle I felt puzzled. I questioned if she had received the word or really understood me. She seemed benumbed.

I said, "Lord, did I say it right? Did I confuse her, or get your word wrong?"

Jesus replied, *You're job is done, now it's between me and her.*

I had become accustomed to giving a prophetic word and seeing people respond immediately. But this time I saw zero response. Many fears and doubts arose in my mind, but I thought, "No. I trust Jesus. I did my job, now it's His turn." It took me weeks to release the 'no response' situation to Jesus, but finally, I did.

Three months later, a female leader at church approached me and started talking about the lady I had given a word to. I wondered how she knew, because I hadn't told anybody. She further stated this lady I prayed with had been attending a Bible study at church.

The church leader's next words explained it all. The other night, she'd stood and shared her testimony. She said, "A girl had prayed with her at church. Initially, she had no idea what she was supposed to do, or what the scripture had meant. As she continued through the Bible study, the Lord revealed areas where she'd been harboring past pain. She thought her past issues had been resolved. She had gone to counseling and life seemed good. But she'd been blind to how deep those wounds cut. She felt thankful for the word released to her because now Jesus was actively walking her through the process of deliverance and healing."

I was astonished. Though it had taken a while, she had her encounter with Jesus. I was so grateful for her breakthrough and that God used me to deliver a message. I learned as followers of Christ, we are used to deliver His mail, packages, and presents.

It's truly a blessing to distribute gifts, but we don't always get to see people's response when they open them. As a mailman, it's not our job to *wait and watch* people open their mail. We don't *make* them open it, show them *how* to open it, or tell them *when* to open it. Once the package leaves our hands, it's between them and the Lord. Our job with that particular package is done. As we keep moving forward, jumping rock to rock, Jesus will give us more gifts to deliver.

Those are a few examples of me learning to use my faith muscles to jump. As I continue venturing along the path of my destiny, my jumps have become bigger and scarier. To date, my most difficult jump was in my last year of graduate school. I knew I was going to open a clinic, but I'd only shared it with my husband and a few close friends. I'm an introvert. I struggle with pleasing people, as well as feelings of inadequacy. I didn't feel smart enough, qualified, or experienced enough to open a clinic. I didn't know a thing about business or starting a non-profit. These are issues God overcame while I was in graduate school.

During that year, everybody asked what I'd be doing after graduation. I wasn't yet confident of my destiny. So, I always replied I'd be involved with mission work. That was my safe answer. I'd then change the subject.

The Lord, however, started nudging me to talk about the clinic. I didn't want to. There were too many unknowns and I didn't have all the answers. I didn't want to answer professionals with a response of "I don't know." The first step was to tell my step-dad. He's a businessman and very intelligent. I knew he'd have good questions. If I could answer him honestly and with faith, then I could tell anybody.

I sat down with my parents and told them about the clinic. I received many questions as suspected and replied, "I don't know, but I trust Jesus won't lead us astray. When it's time to move, He'll show us." It felt freeing. With this conversation, I finally believed I didn't have to know all the answers because Jesus did. He's the one establishing the clinic. The weight is on Him, not me.

People continued to ask about my plans after graduation. I'd say, "I want to open a clinic in town, and eventually run mission teams around the world."

The more I spoke about it, the more my inadequacy shrank. Some said, "That's nice, but what do you *really* want to do?"

I'd allow myself a puzzled look, and repeat, "I'm going to open a clinic. That's all I know."

Those conversations ended quickly. This happened often. But the more I stood in faith, the more I believed it.

After establishing the clinic's board, I started talking to people in the community. Many were excited and wanted to help, but a few made me feel the size of a flea. Though I felt intimidated at times, I learned to release this to the Lord. Some people wouldn't see the vision unless Jesus opened their eyes. I had to trust He'd bring the right people to support the mission, and He did!

From the time of our first board meeting to opening day, only nine months had passed. We obtained everything we needed to open our doors. The Lord showed up and established the clinic. It's completely in His hands and this is only the beginning! I'll continue walking, running, resting, jumping, and enjoying my journey.

Be encouraged and know faith takes time to cultivate. It's like a six-pack of abs. You can't just imagine and desire it, and then it appears. You have to go to the gym and work out. Change your diet. Over time, you'll see ab muscles, but you must continue exercising them. It's the same approach for increasing your faith. Start in the small beginnings. Jump from rock to rock. Give Jesus a chance to show up. Let go of your fears, doubts, and unbelief and leap! Close your eyes and *"Jump Even When You're Afraid."* He'll show up and give you a safe place to land. Keep your eyes fixed on the Lord and walk your destiny.

Lord, I pray for courage and strength. I pray you'd walk us past our fears and give us the confidence to jump into the great unknown. Thank you for always catching us and never letting us fall. You lead us in the way of everlasting and have our best interest in mind. I pray for opportunities to build our faith muscles. Teach us to trust you whole-

heartedly. Thank you for loving us and having a wild

adventure for us to enjoy. I pray for peace and grace over our

minds as we continue along the path of our destiny and learn

to jump with child-like faith!

Blessings,

Kara☺

Oceans of Waiting

The process of strengthening our faith muscles is exciting. Once we see God catch us, we want to keep leaping. It's fun to encounter the Lord and see progress. But sometimes, after the action and adrenaline rush, He'll tell us to *wait*.

Waiting can last from seconds to even years. For me, patience was painful to learn. It felt like every time I turned a corner and entered a new space, Jesus would tell me to sit and wait. I was ready to go on another adventure, but instead I'd submit, and pray for patience. The longer I waited, the more painful it was to endure or keep myself from rushing forward. There were times it felt like an eternity or as if I were crossing an ocean without a paddle.

Looking back over my life, I've waited a long time for the fulfillment of some promises. I'm still waiting for others to be brought to fruition. The hardest part is when the enemy comes to tell lies. He tries to convince me to focus on what I don't have and what hasn't been fulfilled, versus everything the Lord has accomplished. I could feel bitter or angry about what I haven't received. Instead, I choose to be grateful for the grace and love Jesus has shown me throughout life.

One day, I felt downcast. It seemed others around me had been receiving answers to their prayers and having promises fulfilled. I'm truly grateful and happy for people when they receive blessings from the Lord. But, I had slipped into the muck of self-pity. It felt as if the Lord had overlooked and forgotten me. I prayed, reminding Jesus of His promises to my family and the clinic.

These promises seemed out of reach, mostly because I didn't have the resources to make it happen. I tried hanging onto my destiny, but I had trouble conjuring the faith to do so. My emotions plunged me into an abyss of doubt and unbelief.

In that pit, the enemy tormented my mind. I wanted to throw in the towel on everything; my job, the clinic, the book I wanted to write, speaking, and teaching. I told myself I'd take a job in a larger town to make more money. I thought I could make these promises happen through my own labor. But, that was my first mistake. I had the misconception it was my job to fulfill God's promises.

When the Lord gives you a promise, He's responsible for bringing it to fruition. Jesus told me, *Kara, you can labor and toil all you want, but you'll never be able to obtain what I'm going to give you.*

That made no sense to me, and so I considered making life changes to obtain the promises myself. But then, His words sank in. I realized if I tried to accomplish this myself, I'd end up sacrificing family time.

"Alright Lord," I thought. "I won't get a different job. I'll wait, even if it means fewer possessions or living on a tight budget. I won't sacrifice making memories with my family. I'll remain steadfast until you show up and bless me!"

Recently, the Lord directed me to study King David's timeline and write it down. As I read, I noticed King David waited many years to receive his promise. He'd been anointed around the age of fifteen and told he'd be the King of Israel. In a worldly view, he was the least qualified. He was the youngest of his family and tended sheep. The world didn't realize his lowly profession was a training ground that prepared him to walk his destiny and do it well.

Within the next five years, David had been placed to serve under the then King of Israel, King Saul. David found great favor with him, but Saul became jealous of David because Israel honored him for his battlefield successes. Eventually, Saul wanted to kill David. David fled into the wilderness for ten long years.

While being hunted by Saul and his army, David had two chances to take Saul's life. But David had a deep reverence for the Lord and would not kill God's anointed. David wasn't going to supersede God's timing and place himself on the promised platform. Even though David's journey appeared to go in the opposite direction of his destiny, his waiting drew him close to the heart of the Father.

Every step along our journey is necessary for the path ahead. We'll learn and strengthen our spiritual muscles as we continue walking toward our promises.

In the book of Psalms, David poured out his heart to the Lord. There were times David felt doubt, fear, anger, and unbelief. But there were also times he expressed love and thanksgiving to God. David developed such a close relationship with the Lord he felt safe enough to express every emotion. David never questioned God's sovereignty, but communicated his heart with Him. David's dependence on God gave him the courage, faith, and hope to believe His promises despite how desperate his situation appeared. God wants the same relationship with us. In every situation, He desires us to be one hundred percent dependent upon Him.

Life happens. At any time, it can career out of control. When events occur, our heart and our attitudes often conform to our emotions. Pleasurable emotions are easy to manage, but negative emotions are more difficult. Sometimes we feel guilt or shame for feeling a particular way, but we need to give it to the Lord. Like David, it's important to feel and express emotions, but not to lash out or be controlled by them.

If we harbor negativity, our heart may turn toward bitterness, resentment, anger, or even hatred. When expressing negative feelings, we need to have an underlying motive for confession, submission, and hope that Jesus will provide a new perspective to refresh and heal our wounds. Expressing ill feelings should bring freedom within our hearts. It should never be used to judge, condemn, or tear down others. Our part is to express our thoughts, lay them at the foot of the cross, and let the Lord bring us truth, revelation, and clarity.

As David's journey appeared to take him further from his promise, we saw his changeable emotions. He didn't harbor negative emotions, but freely expressed them, and as he did, God brought him spiritual freedom. Fifteen years after being anointed and told his destiny was to be King of Israel, David was anointed King of Judah. It would be an honor, but not his promise. He ruled over Judah for seven and a half years, and then was anointed King of Israel. After waiting twenty-two and a half years, David finally took his place and stood in his promise.

I too, have been waiting for years. The enemy comes at different times and always reminds me what's not happening. But I stay grounded knowing the Lord fulfills promises in His timing, not mine. Whenever I forget, it can darken my heart with self-pity, anger, jealousy, or bitterness. I don't want this to occur, but whenever it does, I turn to Jesus and repent. He then wipes me clean, restoring my hope.

We inherited a kitten. It was originally an inside pet, but she always seemed insistent on going outside, so eventually we let her out. She loved being outdoors. One night, my husband found a couple fleas on her. The next day we went to the store and bought flea shampoo and repellent medicine. Despite the medication, her fleas multiplied and she found herself banished to the garage. We combed her everyday, but kept spotting fleas. It became stressful in our household. We couldn't keep the fleas off her. They continued to multiply and my frustration escalated. I was at my wits end and I pleaded to the Lord, "Can you keep these fleas off her? Nothing seems to work. I don't know what to do."

Jesus replied, *This too shall pass.*

"What are you talking about?" I asked.

He spoke about the bitterness that surfaced in my heart. He said, *Look at the pattern of the fleas. That's how yucky stuff leaks into your heart and tries to take root. Then it becomes difficult to get rid of.*

I envisioned the pattern of the multiplying fleas and received revelation. The fleas had burrowed themselves deep within her fur. Initially, we couldn't see them. Over time, a few exposed themselves so we dug deeper, to the root of the issue. While giving her a bath, we found even more fleas.

That's how negativity works in our hearts. With stealth, it enters our hearts. Within days, it takes root and multiplies. As it compounds, the effects can ripple through to others. I pictured my sinful attitude, as a dandelion after it turns white. When my negativity is released through actions and words, it's like wind blowing the dead seeds of pessimism to others. Then the shards take root in their hearts and weeds grow.

As our household became stressful during our flea fighting, I saw my bitterness and negativity filter down to my children. They were on edge and bickered for no apparent reason. It crushed my heart to see my children react to my root of anger. I turned to God and repented. I asked Him to give me hope, peace, joy, and love while ridding the fleas from our cat. God showed up and answered my prayers. Not immediately, but He did!

During periods of waiting and not seeing my promises fulfilled, there have been times my heart turned bitter. But after reading about King David's journey, how long he waited, and studying his emotional utterances, my hope was restored. My prayers changed. I prayed for the Lord to help me enjoy every moment of my journey and invest quality time in the ones I love. I don't want to rush through life, but find the blessings in everything. Even waiting.

Eleven years ago, I began to walk the path of my destiny. I sought God with all my heart. Six years later, I received a vision for the clinic. Its doors wouldn't open for another four and a half years. The clinic isn't fully standing in the promise, but I know we're on our way.

When I feel discouraged, I pray: "This is what you've promised. I'll remain steadfast and keep my hope and trust in you. No matter how I feel, I believe you'll fulfill the promise in due time. During the wait, please give me patience to be obedient and submit to your timing."

Don't listen to the lies and torments of the enemy. Choose to believe Jesus and His promises for you. Believe the One who speaks life into motion. Be patient and know your time is coming. He hasn't forgotten or missed you. He doesn't give false hope. When the Lord speaks, it's going to happen. There will be times when nothing feels tangible and all appears impossible. Stand strong on your faith muscles. Remember, faith makes a fool of logic.

Look at Noah. God told him to build an ark. Noah spent years building a huge boat that was approximately one and a half football fields long, seventy-five feet wide, and forty-five feet high.

I'd love to have insight into Noah's thoughts while he built the ark. Do you think Noah was always cheerful, happy, and never faced any ridicule or opposition? I imagine there were times he wrestled with God just like we do. Next, are a few words I envisioned Noah speaking to God.

"Is it really going to rain enough to get this ark off the ground? Maybe a small kayak or row boat, but an ark ... really?"

"This is crazy! Is it necessary to build an ark this big? Maybe, I should make it a little smaller?"

"I give up! It's too hard to keep going. Besides, there hasn't been rain for months."

"Everyone walks by and makes fun of me. They say I'm crazy to spend all my time, money, and resources building a huge ark. They say it'll take years of raining before it floats. Are you sure I heard you correctly?"

Despite Noah's uncertainty, opposition, and harassment from the enemy, he used his faith muscles and stood steadfast. He submitted and walked in obedience to God. In the end, it saved mankind. Noah and his family were saved from the floodwaters.

When you're in an ocean of waiting, pray for grace to enjoy it. It's a beautiful place. Rest, as you wait for Jesus to move the waters and lead you to dry land. He promises to guide us, but we don't know the route He'll take. Relax and ride the wave.

As we rest on the raft of His strength, we could try using our hands to paddle. But after a while, we're exhausted and not sure which direction to go. Just wait. Don't race ahead. That will only make your journey more difficult and tiring.

There'll be many unknowns drifting on open waters. Storms or sharks could come along, making our giants resurface.

They might intimidate us, trying to steal our hope. Cry out to God. Hand over to Him your discouragement. He speaks, and the raging waters become still. All torment flees. He'll protect us and provide everything we need while we wait.

Sometimes other ships may come along and offer to give us a ride. Be careful. Know when the Lord has you in a season of waiting, you must wait. While establishing the clinic, people would offer suggestions or ideas. Most times, I didn't get confirmation from Jesus. So I thanked them for their input, telling them I'd pray about it. In the meantime, I wouldn't make any decisions. I waited for direction.

I felt okay waiting and not seeing movement all the time. I believe when I don't see progress, the Lord's plans are moving supernaturally. Unseen. He's quietly preparing the next stage. I'm not going to force my own platform, but I'm going to wait for Jesus to call me forward. Sometimes it feels like an eternity, but **"I'll Wait and Endure the Pain of Patience."** I know it's going to be worth it! I don't want to bless myself. I want the Lord to bless me.

Lord, I pray for patience to be released over us right now, in Jesus' Name. Give us discernment to know when to move and when to wait. Renew our minds to see and think with your perspective. Renew a steadfast spirit within us to endure the pain of patience. Help us enjoy our journey of crossing the ocean and teach us to ride the wave. Build our confidence to know you're with us, even when things seem impossible. You are our provider and the One who makes a way in the desert, and brings water in the wastelands. We trust you and thank you for unfailing love.

Blessings,

Kara☺

Harvest

Walking the path of our destiny is a wild and exciting ride. But there are many obstacles that will come and try to divert us from our route. You must keep your eyes fixed on Jesus and know your promises. Stand firm, because in due time, you'll reap a harvest for everything you've sown.

During my quiet time, I continued to come across scripture that referred to olives. For example, the Mount of Olives, olive trees, and olive oil. Something stirred within me. I decided to learn its significance, see if there were any meanings, and how they might be related. After some research, I realized I wanted my life to reflect that of an olive tree.

Olives are significant because oil is pressed from them. Historically, olive oil had emerged as one of the main staples of life. It had many uses. Ancients used it in cooking, fuel for lamplight, medicinal purposes, and anointing themselves and others. It symbolized peace, righteousness, prosperity, and the power of the Holy Spirit. Olive trees produce beautiful and sacred fruit. But it requires a torturous procedure for both the tree and it's offspring to obtain olive oil.

This process reminds me of walking the path of my destiny. I aspire to be a vessel and disciple for Jesus. I want to produce fruit that reflects His heart. But, I must first go through an enduring process in order to produce "oil" for Jesus.

Olive trees have distinct characteristics. They survive in either warm or cool weather. They can grow in variable terrains: grassy hills, valleys, or rocky mountainsides. These differing regions remind me of seasons of life. Some are grassy hills, which are fun, pleasant, and exciting. Other times, the Lord takes us to the valleys, rocky grounds, or deserts. I envision my rough terrains as times of training. When I submit to the season, there's always a lesson to learn. I now consider hard ground a blessing because it forges something deep within my soul, making me more like Jesus. Just as the olive tree thrives in every terrain, my desire is to richly produce fruit, every season.

Olive trees won't produce fruit until they've grown an average of five years. This reminds me of laboring and waiting. These trees may seem worthless, but in time, they reveal fruit.

Sometimes, the Lord leads us to a place that doesn't appear to be heading toward our promises. This might raise questions or doubt in our minds. But, if God leads you somewhere, submit. Although we may not initially see the fruit of our labor, in time, we will. I view the duration of laboring as a time of testing. It makes me evaluate my true motives. Am I doing this for the reward, or because I love Jesus?

When I labored to establish the clinic, I didn't see any fruit for a while. The Lord told me, *You build it and I'll bring the people.*

Our team worked hard and obediently to establish the clinic. We opened, then waited for clients. Initially, it was very slow. During our first six months we had days we saw no patients. It was discouraging. I had to shift my focus to what the Lord was doing. I knew there had to be a purpose and reason. But what? Looking back, our true motives were being tried.

Although we had very few clients, our job was to be faithfully obedient to Jesus. Would we use our time wisely? Would we be available? Would we get discouraged and leave? During this time, we had volunteers quit. Yet, it became a significant time to build the ministry into the heart of the clinic. We now have a small team of volunteers who are learning to flow with the Spirit. They're trained to help carry the mantle for the clinic. The number of patients still fluctuates. But, when the number is low, it's time for us to labor in a different area. I know the Lord's giving us space to do so. In time, we'll see what we're laboring for and celebrate our first fruits.

Besides years of laboring to produce fruit, the olive tree must also endure pruning. It consists of cutting off damaged, diseased, and rotten branches. Sometimes branches are co-dominant. One branch needs to be removed, or it'll keep the tree from reaching it's full potential. Pruning is beneficial. But when performed incorrectly, it harms the tree.

In life, pruning is painful! The co-dominant branch reminds me of our flesh versus God. We must allow the Lord to prune us, so His light will shine through us. He performs this in phases. He doesn't just cut the whole branch off the first swipe. Many times, He begins on the outer part of the branch and works His way toward the trunk.

Pruning allows the Lord to illuminate any darkness inside my heart. I don't always realize I'm operating in pride, selfish ambition, or offense. Once I'm aware, He'll begin the process of clipping away unhealthy branches. These growths drain me of life, and don't allow the character and heart of the Lord to shine through me.

Last summer, Jimmy was repairing ductwork under our house. He noticed our crawl space was damp, but didn't look further into the issue. Months later, I noticed the paint on our shower was starting to bubble. I mentioned it to my husband and we agreed to investigate the cause while replacing the bathtub.

We subsequently found moisture, but still no cause. Since the space was open and empty, Jimmy decided to replace all the pipes. In doing so, he found the drainpipe had eroded. So every time we'd showered or drained the tub, it leaked under our house.

This is how the Lord prunes our hearts. First, we must go through the process of Him cleaning out the messy stuff. Then we can begin to see the issues at the core of our heart that produce dead, weak, or diseased fruit. Next, Jesus prepares our hearts to receive the blessings and next steps on our journey. Like removing an eroded pipe in order to lay the groundwork for a new bathtub and shower. This is part of the first fruits of the pruning process.

A full harvest isn't possible until olive trees have been cultivated for eight to twelve years. When these trees have fully matured and the crop is ripe, it's time to gather the yield. To gather the olives, the tree and its limbs are shaken or beaten with sticks, knocking them to the ground.

As followers of Jesus, we've chosen a difficult path. The Bible tells us we will endure hardship. But we have the promise God is always with us.

There will be times we'll be beaten or bruised. Because of the cross, we can overcome any shaking. Like everyone, I've been wronged in life. It's hard not to hold offense, especially when I felt I had every reason to. But only God can heal my heart. I know I've forgiven others when I don't want to cringe or roll my eyes upon hearing their names.

When Jesus hung on the cross He cried out, *"Father, forgive them, for they do not know what they are doing."* *(Luke 23:24)*

He pleaded to the Father to forgive these men who beat, wrongly accused, and nailed Him to a cross. Every time I'm reminded of this passage, I realize the times I've been wronged are nothing in comparison. I've never been mistreated like Jesus, and if He can ask forgiveness for His offenders, then so can I.

Naturally, my flesh craves revenge, but my spirit rejects it, because vengeance only produces rotten fruit. Forgiveness isn't saying you're weak, or the other person is right. It's taking a stance that you're not going to let their wrongdoing hold you in bondage. I may convince myself it's no big deal or it's in the past, but my heart still feels the pain. The only way to walk in full forgiveness is to give it to God and let Him bring healing. Once healing starts, our fruit is ready for harvest.

Once the olives are gathered, there's still a lengthy process to procuring oil. The olives are crushed in a press or trodden by barefoot people. In the New Testament Paul states, **"We are hard pressed on every side, but not crushed; perplexed, but not in despair; persecuted, but not abandoned; struck down, but not destroyed. We always carry around in our body the death of Jesus, so that the life of Jesus may also be revealed in our body. For we who are alive are always being given over to death for Jesus' sake, so**

that his life may also be revealed in our mortal body. So then, death is at work in us, but life is at work in you." (2 Corinthians 4:8-12).

Like the olive, we are pressed and crushed to extract the rich oil. As we die to the desires of our flesh, we produce the fruit of Christ. Trials arise in life. There's no way to prevent them. Christians are a witness to others by how we respond to tragedy, pain, chaos, and destruction. Trials are hard to endure. But God gives us strength to survive the press, producing pure fruit.

After extraction, olive oil is initially bitter. It needs fermentation, which takes a few days to a few months. After this process, the oil is ready for use. This curing process points out the purifying grace of the Holy Spirit. Left to ourselves, we are bitter fruit. But with seasoning, we become rich and resourceful oil.

We can never be perfect, nor were we created to handle glory or fame. However, the Holy Spirit shows us how to glorify the Father in all we say and do. This life isn't about us. It's about a loving and gracious Father who wants an intimate relationship with us. One day, He wants to bring us all home to live with Him forever.

The olive tree is faithful, producing fruit every year. It's willing to be beaten and shaken in order to yield fruit and oil. As olive trees mature, their trunks become thicker, knotted, and twisted. They are forming into their own unique creation. No olive tree is exactly the same. As the trunk grows and thickens, the insides become hollow. I want my life to reflect that image. As I continue to spiritually mature, I empty out the desires of my flesh and make space for the Holy Spirit to fill me.

You'll eventually see a bountiful harvest. Not only the olive, but the offspring it produces. As you look at the base of a mature olive tree, you'll see shoots growing from the roots. Each tree averages five to ten shoots. Olive trees live for centuries. But when one dies, or is cut down, its shoots continue growing because the roots are grounded in the same fertile soil.

As a parent, my shoots are my children. My hope is that my kids will be forever rooted in Jesus. I want them to mature, becoming their own creation, producing their own fruit, and making spaces for their own shoots to grow. It's been a long journey, sowing and then waiting for the harvest. But it's worth the wait. We're now reaping some of the first fruits of the planting, and it's beautiful!

Our children give us little reminders of the seeds our family is sowing. It's an honor to teach them Kingdom concepts. Our desire as parents is to give our kids a higher platform to start from than we did. We want our ceiling to be their floor. We desire for them to be more and do more for the Kingdom than us.

Only part of our harvest is sown into our children. We sow seeds everywhere: at a restaurant, church, friend's house, or the mall. We're to represent Christ in all we do. It can be as simple as saying "Thank You" or holding a door open. People don't always remember the words we say, but they remember the way our love and compassion made them feel.

Jesus is love. You can't have love without action. I can talk about my love, but if my actions don't align with my words, they are meaningless.

I haven't always sown good seeds. Some have been beautiful, but some were rotten. The rotten fruit grew from seeds of selfish ambition, jealousy, offense, or bitterness. I'm not proud of it, but it's part of my story. My turning point was in college. My fluctuating life habits made me miserable. I felt like broken pottery, my pieces scattered, and no way to put them back. Only Jesus could mend me, fitting the pieces together in a more perfect design. In my desperation, I sought out Jesus, and He answered me.

I desire to bear good fruit. I'm ashamed of the rotten fruit I've produced in the past. Now, I choose to lay my heart before the Lord daily, to be refined. The fruit I reap is worth the fire. Jesus gives me seeds to sow and my harvest is seeing Him encounter others while restoring their hope and joy.

I believe God wants each of us to yearn to be like the olive tree. He has beautiful oil He wants us to produce and release. Don't be weary or discouraged along your journey because your labor is not in vain. Soon you'll see what you're laboring for, and in time, you'll reap a bountiful harvest. I **"Give Thanks to the Lord Daily"** for the journey He's taken me on. It's been hard and He's tested my faith, but I've developed a stronger hope, trust, and love for God. Even when things appeared to be a disaster, I've seen Him work things out for my good. For these life experiences I'm forever grateful. I'll continue to submit, emulating the life of an olive tree. I've seen glimpses of its fruit and my life will never be the same!

Lord, thank you for your great grace and mercy. Thank you for seeing past our external appearance and looking deep into our hearts and seeing who you created us to be. I pray for an awakening in hearts right now in Jesus' Name to rise to the call you've placed on our lives. I pray for a desire within us to live a life like the olive tree. We empty ourselves out to have more of you. I pray for willing hearts to go through the press. I pray for a harvest beyond what our minds can fathom. Please give us the strength, endurance, and hope to keep laboring, knowing You are our true reward! We lay our heart of gratitude and appreciation before you, because you are molding us into a beautiful masterpiece.

Blessings,

Kara☺

Testimony

Throughout this book, you've seen parts of my story unfold. It's my Cinderella story of being transformed from rags to riches. My riches aren't material things, but are the riches within my heart that nothing can take away or destroy. I'm rich because I've encountered the love of Jesus. There's nothing more precious than Him.

I pray as you have read this book you'll know you can be accepted into the Kingdom. Life is messy. We all have a story. We all have things from our past we're not proud of. But we have a Savior who bore our sins and stood in the gap, allowing us into his royal family.

Walking the path of our destiny, we're tried and tested. That's what builds our *Test*-imony. Our story is how Jesus showed up in our lives. As followers of Jesus, we have a mandate on our lives to be His hands and feet. We're called to action. It's time to get off the sidelines and get into the game. The Lord is on the move and He's in the business of winning hearts. He's invited us to take part in His master plan. Just like any sporting event, you can read the rulebook, but you can't win the game until you play. Sometimes "religion" can deteriorate to following rules, but Jesus didn't say follow religion. He said, *Follow me.* He put His heart into motion. When we get into the game, we share our testimony about Jesus rescuing us from the pit of destruction.

It doesn't matter where you are along the path of your destiny. You have a story to share. You may not know Jesus, but maybe you're a little curious. Open your heart and talk to Him like you would another person. Ask him to be Savior of your life. Ask him to encounter you and wait until He does. That's your story. What led you to wonder about Jesus? What happened as you talked to Him? That's what people need to hear. They need to understand, no matter how messed up their life, Jesus loves them.

Your story has a beginning. But the end isn't until you take your last breath and enter into eternity. There, you have reached your destination. Walking the path of your destiny builds chapters within your story. Some chapters you haven't experienced yet, but you're on your way to writing them. Tell others the chapters that are already written. The longer we walk with Jesus, the more stories we'll have. These testimonies are our treasures. They are too important to *not share.*

It's time for us to get into the game and become a disciple for the Lord! When life ends, what really matters? Is it the house, car, bank account, or how many vacations we've taken? No. It's about our relationship with Jesus and other people. Life is about being a disciple for Christ.

As I'm writing this, I'm reminded of the parable in the Bible about the three men and bags of gold. (Matthew 25:14-30) Jesus tells a story of a boss who's going on a journey. He wants his servants to care for his wealth. He gives the first servant five bags of gold, the second servant two bags, and the third servant one bag. Over time, the boss returns and settles accounts with his servants. The first man returned his master's investment twice over, for a total of ten bags. The second also doubled his bags, totaling four. The boss was pleased with the return, blessing both men. The third man approached, giving the master his original bag of gold. He claimed he knew the boss was a hard man, so he was afraid, and buried his bag in the ground. He had no return investment from what he was given. The master was angry and called him a lazy servant. The master took his bag, giving it to the first man who had ten bags of gold.

Once we enter into relationship with Jesus, He deposits gold within our hearts. As we venture along our journey, we learn to recognize and use these treasures. We have the choice to hide them and keep them for ourselves, or share them with the world. When we share our story, we're investing our treasures in others. We're being good stewards of our God given resources and blessings. We're talking about the messy places in our lives and how Jesus brings restoration.

You don't have to be a pastor or involved with a ministry to talk about Jesus. Your platform is right where you are, the people you encounter on a day-to-day basis. These include people at our job, church, family, and neighborhood. Be obedient with those the Lord places in your path and He'll continue to expand your platform.

As we share our story with others, seeds are planted. When these "gardens" journey through life, they'll meet others who will water and plant even more seeds. Some day, their hearts will bloom and they'll be ready to walk with Jesus.

We aren't responsible for saving souls. Jesus is. No human being can be credited with saving people from condemnation. We may have the honor of praying with people to receive Jesus, but the glory isn't ours.

Glory *always* goes to God. Understand, that when we share our story, we're not the hero. We're telling the story of how the Hero saved us. Our testimony is to encourage others and explain how Jesus wants to be in relationship with them.

Working at the hospital, I dreaded twelve-hour shifts. The only thing that made it worthwhile was whenever I witnessed Jesus encounter someone. Driving to work, I'd pray for my heart to be opened, allowing the Lord to use me. I dreaded one particular day because we had a full census, which meant beds were filled to capacity. Yet, I had hope because I'd decided to step onto the playing field. I wanted to join the game.

The day was busy as predicted, but eventually I had some downtime and decided to complete one of my college assignments. My homework required me to ask someone how their religious beliefs played a role in their overall health status. Only one patient was available to talk, so I asked if I could interview her.

I was nervous because I didn't know if she practiced Christianity. I wasn't yet confident sharing my faith with others, especially without knowing their beliefs. I stepped into my fear and started asking questions. She believed in Jesus and spoke freely of her faith. My anxiety evaporated. I was encouraged because she wasn't afraid to tell me about the Lord. Our conversation went beyond my assignment when she told me her life story. This woman had been through a lot, being sick and in the hospital. She was on antibiotics, but would likely need major surgery if the medicine didn't work.

By the end of our conversation, I felt the Holy Spirit nudging me to pray for her. I didn't want to. My mind listed every excuse why I shouldn't. Other staff members needed me, so our conversation ended. When exiting her room, I assisted her to the bathroom. As soon as I closed the door, I heard the

Lord say, *When you come back to help her to the chair, ask her if you can pray for her.*

When her call light turned on, I went and met her at the bathroom door. I looked at her and spoke of what had happened when I walked out of her room. I then asked, "So, can I pray for you?"

She smiled. "As soon as the bathroom door shut, I heard Jesus tell me, *You need to ask this girl to lay hands on you and pray.* So let's do this," she said.

I put one hand on her abdomen and held her other hand while I prayed. For the first time ever, I felt the anointing released *through* me. I could feel something like electric bolts of energy and my hands felt really warm. It was weird, but so exciting! I looked at her and explained what I'd just felt.

She said, "I felt it and I received it." In my spirit, I knew the Lord was going to heal her. I just didn't know how.

A few months later, while beginning my shift at the hospital, I reviewed my list of patients. To my surprise, I recognized the name of the woman I prayed for earlier. I couldn't wait to see her.

When I walked in her room, I smiled with excitement. "What happened? Did the Lord heal you?"

"Yes!" she replied. "I went to surgery because according to the radiology tests, the infection hadn't resolved. Afterward, the surgeon removed my appendix, but he didn't find any infection."

I was ecstatic and so grateful to have been a part of her story. She also said she'd been telling everybody what the Lord had done for her, and what a rippling effect it had on other people.

These stories are inspiring, but know every believer has access to the Holy Spirit and He wants to work through you. Testimonies are available for every disciple. The enemy tries to tell us otherwise, but he speaks lies. He'll do anything to keep us from walking in the fullness of who God created us to be. Take a step and get on the field. Maybe it's your first time or maybe you've been sitting on the sidelines for a while. It's time to rise up. There are many broken people in this world and they need stories of hope.

Walking the path of my destiny has allowed me to share many true events. As you travel through life, you'll develop an abundance of testimonies. Don't keep them for yourself, but shout from the mountaintops what the Lord has done for you. Your stories will continually build, and you'll realize Jesus has been writing your story all along.

I didn't always attend church when I was young. But I recall people who have helped me along my faith walk. They didn't necessarily talk about Jesus, but demonstrated His heart. I'll never forget key moments where I felt the heart of the Lord.

Initially, I didn't know what I was experiencing. I just thought they were nice people. As I look back, it was Jesus encountering me through them, even though I didn't yet know Him. I now realize throughout my whole life, He's been giving me the message that He's with me.

Nothing speaks to people's hearts better than an experience. God wants to give you opportunities to encounter His love. God loves us fiercely. He wants nothing more than our hearts to receive His love and every good thing He has prepared for us.

I may lack the verbal skills to fully express God's love, but I can't keep quiet. I'll continue to get into the game and "**Share My Story**." Will you join me? Go. Share your story. *Chase Your Destiny*!

Thank you for your love. It's better than life and everything we live for. When you fill us from the inside out, we can't contain it. We have to release it to others. I pray for a supernatural filling of our hearts to be like you. I pray for restoration in people's voices. Anything that would try to constrict or keep us from sharing your love I bind in Jesus' Name. Thank you for encountering us and giving us a testimony. Call forth your players to get into the game! Thank you for allowing us to be vessels, it's truly an honor.

Blessings,

Kara☺

My Treasures

1. Serving and Loving Others

2. Medicine is my Ministry

3. Run my Race

4. I'm in Process and that's Okay

5. I will be Part of Overseas Missions

6. Create Space to Breathe

7. Jump Even When You're Afraid

8. I'll Wait and Endure the Pain of
    Patience

9. Give Thanks to the Lord Daily

10. Share My Story

Additional Acknowledgements

I'd to thank my editor, Monica. Your encouragement and assistance was much appreciated. You have a way with words and have helped make the words of this book come alive. Thank you from the bottom of my heart for believing in me and the message I had to release!

Roger and Nancy Thompson, you both have been such an inspiration to me. You two are great role models and your heart for the Lord is evident. Thank you for your support and encouragement throughout the establishment of the clinic and the publishing of this book. You're both a blessing to me!

Ashley Bailey, thank you so much for your editing work and honest feedback. I'm so thankful I've had the opportunity to get to know your sweet, generous, and fun-loving personality.

Special thanks to my family, friends, and clinic volunteers for encouraging me to keep moving forward. You've all been an inspiration to me and I'm grateful for each of you.

End of Book

Thank you for reading Chasing Your Destiny. I hope you are encouraged and know you were created for a reason. You have an assignment and a key role in God's redemptive plan. Come as you are and seek God with your whole heart. Then watch Him work through you!

In June 2017, a Chasing Your Destiny Workbook will be available for purchase. This workbook will help you map out your own journey and see that God has always been for you.

In addition to writing, I offer Author Presentations and am willing to teach a weekly Bible Study. If you'd like having me as a guest speaker/teacher, it would be my pleasure to see if I can accommodate you.

Please Contact me at:

Kara.mankey@unfailingloveclinic.org

For information on Unfailing Love Clinic visit:

www.unfailingloveclinic.org

Blessings!